Tan Rosie® Caribbean Kitchen

by Monica Cudjoe &
Lee Sylvester

This edition published in 2016 by Tan Rosie Foods Ltd
Tan Rosie Foods Ltd
PO Box 15865
Birmingham
B23 3JB
UK

©Copyright 2016 text, photography and design: Lee Sylvester & Monica Cudjoe,
Tan Rosie Foods Ltd
www.tanrosie.com
Email: info@tanrosie.com

Follow Tan Rosie on twitter: twitter.com/tanrosie
Like us on Facebook: facebook.com/tanrosie

Text: Lee Sylvester & Monica Cudjoe
Photography: Lee Sylvester
Designer: Lee Sylvester

ISBN 978-0-9572771-3-7

You can buy this book directly from the publisher at www.tanrosie.com
This book is also available to download in ebook format from Amazon.com or
Apple iBooks at the iTunes Store.

acknowledgements

We all have to eat, that is a necessary need to continue living. So why not try and make eating as interesting and enjoyable as we possibly can. In so doing we need to create the most taste bud tantalising foods as we possibly can. To this end this is what we try to achieve when creating this book of recipes.

In putting together this collection of recipes we draw heavily on on our traditional family heritage, inspirations from our travels through the Caribbean and my twist on some classics. In creating these dishes we needed some testers!

I am grateful to my children Jeremy and Lee for their honest critique of the finished products. Their input was well appreciated. To my sister Jane who was also co opted into the tasting sessions, much gratitude. To my niece, Amani for all her help.

A big thank you to all who came for the final session of tastings come Sunday lunch, Elizabeth and her son Joel, Verna, Esther, Remi, Merry and son Nile, Afia and her lovely mum Rukhsana. Thank you all for your wonderful support and encouragement.

Monica Cudjoe, Tan Rosie.

Thank you to Aunty Jane for the use of her camera to complete this book! Jeremy, Remi and Amani thanks for helping out at the food festivals and farmers markets. Thank you to my dad Charles for the constant encouragement and advice. A special thank you to my mom Monica for sharing her delicious recipe ideas and cooking techniques.

Lee, K Sylvester, Tan Rosie.

contents

introduction..7

a-z caribbean fruit & vegetables................9

essential caribbean cooking tips...........33

bakery...37

1 pot dinners...59

meat & poultry...69

fish dishes..91

vegetarian dishes...................................107

side dishes..127

salads..145

desserts..159

drinks..179

menu ideas...189

glossary..201

index...205

introduction

Thank you purchasing our latest book! With this new collection of recipes we aim to show you how to cook our favourite dishes from "back home" and we also feature new and exciting creations using a varitey of Caribbean ingredients.

Many of these recipes were originally cooked at our successful Supper Club in our home in Birmingham which we've been running for 6 years. At the Supper Club we feature an array of interesting and tasty dishes from around the Caribbean, with a vision to showcase the varied cuisine you can find on these islands and can't necessarily find in a restaurant in the UK. It's not just about rice and peas and jerk chicken you know!

Food has always brought our family together from birthday celebrations to family BBQ's in the summer. We've always had a passion for food and love exploring different Caribbean islands on our travels. We love travelling to the Caribbean and enjoy eating local food in family restaurants, as it's here, where you'll find the true taste of Caribbean.

Caribbean cuisine is "fusion" foods made up of African, Spanish, Portuguese, Chinese, Indian, Native Taino & Arawaks to name a few. Contrary to popular belief, Caribbean food is not all hot and some islands do not use chilli in their dishes at all.

Many islands use some of the same ingredients in their cuisine, but they are used in different ways to create their traditional dishes. For instance, St Lucians do not have rice and peas as a complete dish - they tend to serve the rice seperately to the peas and then use a different variety of peas (or beans). Grenadians use pigeon (or gungo) peas compared with Jamaicans who use kidney beans for their rice and peas dishes. Trinidadians & Tobagoans love their hot pepper sauce and have a strong Indian influence in their food. Grenadians would never use ackee in their salt fish dishes, as the ackee fruit does not generally grow on the island. There are many similarities and differences in Caribbean food culture of which we explore in this book.

We've included a couple of interesting chapters on Caribbean ingredients and how to use them and essential cooking tips for creating that authentic Caribbean taste. We hope you'll find these informative and they should give you the confidence to experiment with new ingredients to create the Caribbean dishes you've always wanted to make.

Monica & Lee

caribbean
fruit, vegetables
& spices

caribbean fruit, vegetables & spices.

The Caribbean boasts a huge variety of delicious fruit, vegetables, herbs and spices. Take a look at some of the produce available across these islands.

vegetables

ACKEE - grows on trees and is found all over Jamaica. It's very poisonous when unripe. When ripe, the fruit splits to show three large black seeds, yellowish flesh and when cooked it resembles scrambled eggs. Make the Jamaican dish ackee & salt fish.

AUBERGINE - also known as egg plant, garden egg or melongene. Great in curries, stuffed, roasted, fried and much more.

BREADFRUIT - a large round, rough skinned vegetable which grows on trees and can weigh up to 4lb. A great source of carbohydrates. Treat like a potato - roast (in the skin too), bbq, mash, bake - you name it!

CALLALOO - the leaves of the Edoe root vegetable. A green vegetable similar to spinach. Treat this like spinach when cooking.

CORN - a staple ingredient in the Caribbean and used to make cornmeal/polenta when dried and milled. Often roasted as a streetfood and used in various dishes.

CHRISTOPHENE/CHO CHO/CHOYOTE - sometimes spelt christophene, a pear-shaped member of the melon family with a pale green skin and flesh which tastes similar to marrow. Use in soups, stews (similar to a potato).

COCO/EDDOE - a hairy root vegetable, about the size of a large potato and similar in taste. Treat like a potato when cooking.

OKRA - a spear shaped green pod, filled with glutinous seeds. When large, it is too fibrous to eat. Very commom in the Caribbean. Use in various ways from frying, stews, soups and in rice dishes etc.

PEAS (PIGEON/GUNGO/BLACK EYE/CHICKPEAS/KIDNEY BEANS ETC) - various types of peas are available in the Caribbean (pictured pigeon peas). They are a staple food used in rice, stews and soup dishes.

PLANTAIN - a member of the banana family. They must be cooked, treat like a potato. Green plantains are unripe and firm - great for making crisps. Yellow plantains are ripe and slightly sweeter, great for making fritters.

PUMPKIN - sometimes known as squash. Can be used in savoury or sweet dishes. Tastes great steamed, mashed, in soups, roasted. Treat like a potato.

SWEET POTATO - available in different varieties, orange flesh and white flesh. The orange flesh potato has a loose consistancy and rich colour. The white flesh potato is firmer in texture great for making chips or crisps.

WALNUTS - available across the Caribbean. Grown on trees.

YAM - a stachy and firm root vegetable often used in soups, stews. Treat like a potato when cooking.

BLUGGOE - a member of the banana family. A vegetale that must be cooked. The outer skin shape is angular and square-like.

CALABASH - a large round vegetable grown on trees. The outer skin can be hollowed and dried to make bowls. The flesh can be eaten.

GREEN BANANA - a member of the banana family and must be cooked. Treat like a potato when cooking. Often eaten in soups, stews, steamed, boiled and eaten as a side dish.

LAKATAN - a member of the banana family and must be cooked. Turns a rich purple/red colour when ripe.

GREEN FIG - a member of the banana family and must be cooked. Small, round and angular shape. St Lucians cook this with salt fish to create a salad.

fruit

AVOCADO - a green or purple skinned fruit available across the Caribbean.

BANANA - they come in all shapes and sizes. Turns yellow when ripe, the sweetness and taste varies across the varieties.

COCONUT - used unripe (green) and ripe (brown). The white meat of the ripe coconut is used grated, toasted or flaked. The milk can me made into cream. Green coconuts contain jelly and water (served as a drink on the beach!) Used extensively in cooking from sweet to savoury dishes.

CUSTARD APPLE - a brown fruit with sweet moist pulp, cream coloured like custard.

GRAPEFRUIT - the same as the European citrus fruit.

GUINEPS/CHENNET - small green fruit with apricot-coloured flesh and one large stone.

GUAVA- small yellow-skinned fruit with pink or yellow flesh and many seeds.

LEMON - very similar to European citrus, but often rough skinned.

LIME - the same as the European citrus fruit. We use limes frequently in cooking, marianding and in drinks.

ORANGES - same as the European varieties but usually with a green/yellow skin colour.

MANGO - grows on large trees, a fruit with greenish-yellow skin. They come in different varieties such as Julies, green and Bombays. Unripe they can be used for chutneys or salads.

MELON - both cantaloup and pink-fleshed water melon.

PAPAYA/PAW PAW - varies in size and flavour. Skin is greenish or yellow when very ripe, flesh is apricot-coloured and delicate with small black seeds.

PINEAPPLE - various sizes and available on many islands.

SAPODILLA/NASBERRY - roughly around the size of an orange. Brown skin with a sweet yellow flesh and several large flat black seeds.

SOURSOP - a large green skinned fruit covered in soft spines. White flesh with black seed in the centre. Can be made into a drink or ice cream.

STAR FRUIT - a yellow skin fruit with a star-like shape.

TAMARIND - brown pod-like firm outer shell fruit, easliy cracked to reveal sweet/citrus brown sticky flesh covering dark brown large seeds. Grown on large trees. Used in all aspects of cooking from drinks to sauces.

POMERAC - when fully ripe the outer will turn a pinky-reddish colour. The texture is similar to an apple and mildy sweet.

SUGAR CANE - tall slim wooden stems which are sweet inside. Usually a green/yellow outer skin with cream fiborous inner. Used to make sugar. Can be pressed to make drinks.

GOLDEN APPLE - about the size of a lemon. Green smooth outer skin, similar to an apple, with yellow firm flesh with small cream seeds. Slight citrus flavour.

CERIS - Similar to cherries. Sweet fruit with large stone.

DAMSEL - Sweet fruit found in clusters on tall trees.

SHADO BENE - Herb often commonly found in Trinidad & Tobago amongst other islands. Similar to coriander. Used as a seasoning and can be made into a sauce for marinading.

COFFEE BEANS - The coffee bean is found all over the Caribbean, roasted and ground.

UGLI FRUIT- a large citrus uneven and thick skinned. Similar to a grapefruit when peeled.

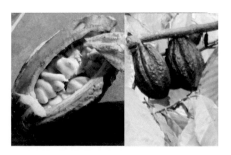

COCOA - yellow-red hard outer skin with mildy sweet white/cream flesh covered seeds with brown beans/seeds in the centre. These brown cocoa beans are dried, fermented and made into chocolate products.

NONI - white/yellow outer skin with wit white flesh. None sweet, bitter flavour. Can be used in drinks.

DATE PALM - red coloured fruit with large seed and sweet flavour. Grown on tall palm trees.

herbs & spices

ALLSPICE/PIMENTO - It's called allspice because it smells slightly of nutmeg, cinnamon and cloves. The berry, the size of a pea, is glossy and black when ripe. It's used in chutneys, marianades and curries.

BAY LEAVES - an evergreen with dark green leaves. Can be used fresh or dried in soups, stews and general marinades.

CHIVE - similar to the spring onion, but with a delicate flavour. Commonly used as a base in Caribbean cooking.

CINNAMON - a sweet spice made from ground tree bark. Used in baking, marinades and much more.

CLOVE - used whole and ground, but very sparingly on a variety of meats, fruits, chutneys and desserts.

GINGER - a bulb-like root which flowers. Used in a variety of dishes. Very good for digestion.

MACE - lacy outer sheath of the nutmeg kernel with a strong nutmeg flavour.

NUTMEG - the stone of the nutmeg fruit. Used in a wide range of dishes from sweet to savoury. Grown extensively in Grenada. Grenada is known as "the spice isle" due to the abundace of nutmeg grown on the island.

PAPRIKA - made from dried sweet pepper and used across meat and fish dishes.

SAGE - plentiful on many islands and used with poultry, pork and fish.

THYME -usually sold in small bunches with chives and parsley tied with a wisp of straw. These are always called "seasonings."

TURMERIC - like saffron and used to colour and flavour rice and curries.

SCOTCH BONNET PEPPER - fiery hot pepper ranging from green, yellow to red in colour - originating in Africa. Used in the Caribbean marinades and as a sauce. In Grenada and Carriacou, they call it "seasoning pepper."

essential caribbean cooking tips

essential caribbean cooking tips

1. Marinade

Most Caribbean meat or fish is marinated before cooking. This gives the meat great depth of flavour and is a must in Caribbean cooking. We usually leave meat or fish to marinade for at least 24 hours in the fridge. I've known some relatives to leave food marinating for 48 hours! If you can't wait that long, we recommend a minimum of 2 hours.

2. Scotch Bonnet Pepper

Contrary to popular belief, not all Caribbean dishes use this famous pepper. It can be used in a variety of ways, but always use caution at first because this little pepper bites back! Why not add a whole scotch bonnet pepper into your curries (make sure you leave it whole) and remove it after cooking – don't let it burst! This will give you the fantastic flavour of the pepper and enough heat to tantalise your taste buds.

3. Coconut Milk

Coconut is a staple ingredient in the Caribbean and it's used in variety of ways in savoury or sweet dishes. Coconut milk (or cream) is superb added to curries. It tastes amazing in soups and of course cakes and sweets. If you are watching your waistline, you can buy low fat coconut milk from most supermarkets. Alternatively, you can make your own low fat version by blitzing fresh coconut pulp with water and straining to create coconut milk.

4. Dutch Pot

Traditional Jamaican cooking utilises the Dutch Pot. It's a large aluminium dome shaped pot and lid which is excellent for making 1-pot dinners, curries and much more. These are available from Caribbean stores or even online. Our family in Carriacou, Grenada have used traditional iron pots over a wood fire in cooking for generations. These days they are mainly used in traditional food festivals on the island such as the Maroon Festival. It's not essential, but a great piece to have!

5. Meat On The Bone

If you really want authentic tasting Caribbean food, you have to use meat on the bone folks. Leave the chicken breasts alone and opt for thighs instead! This is a must – the marrow in the bones adds tremendous flavour to dishes and it's good for you. Once you marinade meat on the bone for 24 hours and cook, your dish will take on a whole new world of flavour. If you have squeamish guests, then remove the bones before serving.

6. Sweet Spices

Sweet spices such as Allspice, Nutmeg and Cinnamon are used in various Caribbean dishes, from sweet to savoury. Our family in Carriacou, Grenada (the spice island) use these spices on a regular basis to give a deeper flavour to our meals. Try adding a teaspoon of allspice to curries. Why not grate fresh nutmeg to your jerk seasoning? It's easy to use these sweet spices in sweet dishes, but try and experiment with savoury dishes too, you'll love it.

7. Sugaring

This is a very traditional technique of Caribbean cooking. It gives meat a luxurious deep brown colour and rich flavour and tastes amazing. Simply add oil to a frying pan, add 2 teaspoons of sugar and heat until brown (but don't burn). Once the sugar has caramelised, add your marinated meat to the pan and cook. This traditional technique is used as a base for stewed dishes and curries. You'll notice a distinct difference in your dishes after using this method for frying off meat. Yum and what a colour!

8. Chives, Thyme, Celery & Scallions

These aromatic herbs and seasoning vegetables are used extensively in Caribbean cooking on many islands. They are often sold in small packages with scotch bonnet pepper in local stores. Add a sprig of thyme to rice and peas to bring out the flavour of the peas or add to soups and stews with a little scotch bonnet pepper!

9. Salted Fish & Meat

Due to the climate, Caribbean people have always preserved meat and fish using salt. Salted fish (or salt fish) is eaten all across the Caribbean in various dishes. The fish is traditionally cod, but there are many different types available in supermarkets for you to try. Salt fish is usually soaked, washed or boiled to remove the salt before cooking. We prefer to soak and wash the fish in several changes of cold water and soak over night. Salted meats are often used in soups and stews which are slow cooked – it gives the dish a rich, tasty flavour. Try it!

10. Ground Provisions

Instead of using your usual Maris Piper potato, why not opt for some Tania, Sweet Potato or Cassava? You can use these vegetables in the same way as your average potato and they taste great too. We always use the white sweet potato when cooking. The white variety tends to hold its shape more and we think it tastes better than the orange sweet potato which can be watery and soft. These vegetables are available from most Asian stores and some larger supermarkets.

bakery

fried bakes or dumplings

Fried bakes or fried dumplings are a staple food within any home in the Caribbean. They are a popular streetfood often served with salt fish or jerk chicken for lunch or as a breakfast dish.

2 Cups self raising flour
50g softened butter
25g sugar
1 tsp salt
Vegetable oil for frying
Warm water

Method:
1. In mixing bowl place first four ingredients and mix to fine bread crumbs.
2. Add water a little at a time until all ingredient are incorporated into a firm dough.
3. Turn dough out onto a floured board and knead for about 5 minutes.
4. Return dough to mixing bowl, cover with with cling film or a damp clean tea towel, keep in a warm place for about 30 minutes.
5. After 30 minutes, turn dough out, divide into 12 equal portions and form into balls.
6. Flatten each ball into 4" circles.
7. Place vegetable oil into frying pan and bring to medium to hot temperature.
8. Place flattened dough into oil and fry for 3 to 4 minutes on either side until golden brown.
9. Remove from oil with slotted spoon and place on tray with kitchen towel to absorb excess oil.
10. Repeat with the remaining dough until all is cooked.
11. Serve while still warm. Eat on their own or serve with salt fish, cheese or jerk chicken!

festivals

Festivals are a Jamaican streetfood snack which can also be eaten for breakfast. They are made from flour and cornmeal with a little sweetness added into the mix. These little beauties are fried and can be eaten with salt fish, jerk pork, jerk chicken you name it! We've made ours slightly smaller in size and they have a crumblier texture making them extra delicious.

2 Cups self raising flour
1 Cup fine corn meal
1 Tsp baking powder
50g softened butter
50g vegetable shortening
1/4 cup sugar

1 Tsp ground cinnamon
1 tsp fine sea salt
1 Tsp vanilla extract
Vegetable oil for frying
Warm Water

Method:

1. Place all dry ingredients in mixing bowl. Then, using hand or fork mix through.
2. Add butter and shortening and mix to fine bread crumbs consistency.
3. Add water to mixture a little at a time until all dry ingredients are incorporated together.
4. Turn out dough onto a floured surface and knead for about 5 minutes until smooth.
5. Return dough to mixing bowl, cover with damp tea towel or cling film and leave to rest for 30 minutes.
6. After 30 minutes divide dough into 24 balls.
7. Roll out into cylindrical shapes about 2 to 3 inches long - the length of your index finger.
8. In large frying pan decant vegetable oil, enough to cover base of pan.
9. Place on heat source to get oil to medium to hot temperature, you know when oil is hot when you put a tiny piece of dough into hot and it bubbles.
10. Place about a third of the festivals in the hot oil and cook for about 4 to 5 minutes on all sides. Turn festivals when beginning to get golden.
11. When golden on all sides and cooked through, using a slotted spoon remove from oil and place on a prepared tray with kitchen paper to drain.
12. Repeat the process with the remainder of festivals

Tips:

1. A food processor can be used to make the dough.
2. Festival are best served warm.
3. Can be stored in freezer.

To Make Cinnamon Festivals:

For an added twist, try rolling some of the finished festivals in a 4 tbls brown sugar and 4 tbs cinnamon (or enough to cover your batch of festivals). They taste just like a Caribbean style doughnut. Yummy!

cinnamon festivals

traditional festivals

dhal puri roti

Dhal puri roti has been eaten in the Caribbean for decades. It was brought over by Indians and incorporated into the diet of Trinidad & Tobago, Grenada and other Caribbean islands. It's made using split peas which are incorporated into the dough, rolled out then cooked. We usually eat them with curry mutton or a hearty stew.

For dough:
2 cups strong plain flour
1 tsp baking powder
50g vegetable shortening
1 tsp sea salt
1 tsp sugar
Warm water to mix

For filling:
1 cup split peas
1 tsp ground turmeric
1/4 tsp sea salt
1/4 tsp black pepper
Water

Dough Method:
1. In mixing bowl place all dry ingredients.
2. Rub in the shortening.
3. Add warm water to form a firm dough.
4. Knead on floured surface for about 5 minutes.
5. Divide dough into 6 equal portions and form into balls.
6. Cover with damp cloth while filling is being prepared.

Filling Method:
1. In saucepan, place split peas, add 1 litre water to pan.
2. Place on heat and bring to boil, turn heat down and simmer for 15 minutes
3. Remove from heat, drain in colander, rinse in cold water.
4. Place drained split peas in food processor with turmeric, sea salt and black pepper.
5. Blend until fine consistency.
6. Decant mixture into a bowl.
7. Leave to cool thoroughly.

To make Dhal Puri Roti:
1. Flatten each dough ball into a circular disc of 5."
2. Place 2 dessert spoon fulls of split pea mixture into centre of dough and close/seal back.
3. Repeat this process until all balls have been filled.
4. On floured surface, roll out dough balls into a 10" circles.
5. Place Tawa or non-stick frying pan onto heat.
6. When hot, place roti in pan, cook until lightly golden brown for 2 to 3 minutes.
7. Turn to other side and cook for 1 to 2 minutes.
8. Remove from pan and place on tray and keep covered with clean tea towel.
9. Repeat process with other dough balls.

homemade bread rolls

Homemade bread rolls are a staple in our home. You will love this simple delicious recipe we've been making for years and we hope you'll enjoy it too.

900g strong plain or bread flour
50g butter
25g vegetable shortening
25g sugar
10g yeast
1 tsp sea salt
450ml milk and water blend

Method:

1. In large mixing bowl place the first 6 ingredients and rub in. Add milk and water a little at a time to form a soft dough.

2. Turn out dough on to floured and knead for 10 to 15 minutes until a smooth consistency is achieved.

3. Return to mixing bowl, cover with cling film or a damp clean tea towel and leave in a warm place for 1 hour or until doubled in size.

4. After an hour, knead again to knock it back to original size.

5. Divide dough into 24 round balls and place on a greased baking tray to proof again for about 30 minutes.

6. Preheat oven to gas mark 7, bake rolls for 35 to 40 minutes.

7. Leave to cool before eating.

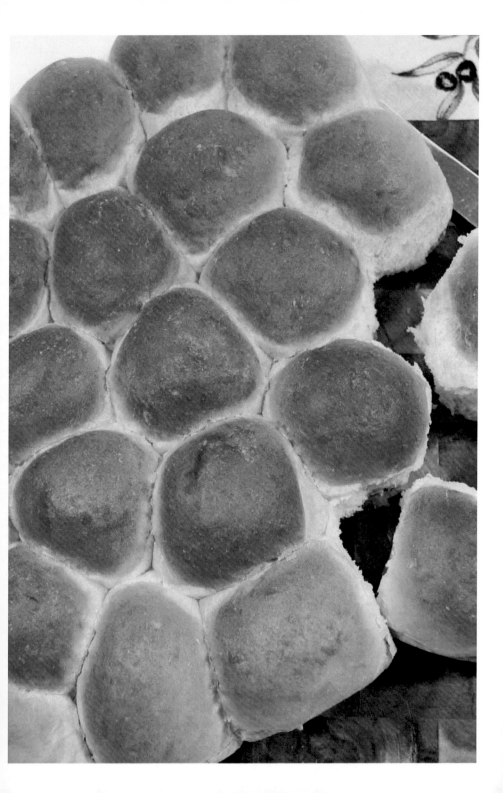

onion flat bread with chilli

We love experimenting with different flavour combinations and this onion flat bread is so easy to make! It tastes even better than the picture and you can make in batches to freeze for future eating.

1/2 cup onions, minced and sauté
in olive oil
2 cups strong plain flour
1 tsp baking powder
1 Tbs scotch bonnet peppers,
minced and saute' in olive oil

1 tsp sea salt
2 tsp sugar
Water to mix

Method:
1. In mixing bowl, place first six ingredients and combine.
2. Add water a little at a time to make firm dough.
3. Turn out on floured surface and knead for 5 minutes.
4. Cover with clean damp cloth or cling film for at least 20 minutes.
5. Divide dough into 6 pieces and form into balls.
6. Roll out balls into 6" to 8" circles.
7. Place frying pan or tawa on heat source.
8. When hot, place rolled out dough and cook for 2 to 3 minutes until golden brown on both sides and cooked through.
9. Turn out on tray and cover with tea towel.
10. Continue process until all flat breads are cooked.

Tips:
These flat breads are great eaten with curries, as a base for a simple cheese and salad sandwich.

banana bread

Banana bread is very popular in Carriacou and many Caribbean islands. It's a great way to use up those over-ripe bananas in a fun way. Banana bread has a sweetness to it and can be eaten on it's own or warm with some butter (or even with a slice of cheese!) It's quick and easy to prepare and tastes delicious.

3 Ripe bananas, crushed
2 Eggs - beaten
2 cups self raising flour
1 tsp baking powder
150g butter - softened

150g light brown sugar
1 tsp vanilla extract
1 tsp ground cinnamon
1/4 tsp grated nutmeg
1/4 tsp sea salt

Method:
1. Preheat oven to gas mark 6.
2. Grease a 9" loaf tin.
3. In mixing a mixing bowl cream butter and sugar until fluffy.
4. Add eggs, butter and sugar mixture a little at a time until all is incorporated.
5. Stir in vanilla extract.
6. Add crushed banana and stir.
7. Add self raising flour, spices and salt.
8. Stir through to incorporate all the dry ingredients, this will take a couple seconds, it is important not to beat too vigorously!
9. Pour batter into greased loaf tin, bake in oven for 1 to 1 hour 15 minutes. After 50 minutes check to determine if loaf is cooked through. This is done by inserting a skewer into bread, if it comes out clean it is cooked. If not leave in oven for a further 15 minutes.
10. Cool on wire rack when removed from oven. Cool before serving.

coconut scones

Whilst travelling through St Lucia, we came across many coconut based bakery dishes. These scones taste amazing as a savoury snack or you can add jams etc to make them a lovely sweet treat.

500g Self raising flour
100g softened butter
2tsp baking powder
50g sugar
1 tsp sea salt
150g grated coconut
150ml coconut milk

Method:
1. Preheat oven to gas mark 7.
2. In a mixing bowl, place flour, salt and butter. Rub in butter to a fine bread crumb consistency.
3. Add sugar, grated coconut and coconut milk.
4. Mix well to form a soft dough.
5. Cover with cling film and allow to rest for 15 minutes.
6. On a floured surface, roll out dough to an 1 inch thickness.
7. Using a pastry cutter cut out scones.
8. Place scones on a greased baking tray, brush with a little milk.
9. Bake in oven on gas mark 7 for 25 minutes until lightly golden brown.

Tip: Serve warm with butter and any jam of your choice. A dollop of whipped cream added makes it extra special!

cassava bread

serves 4 -6

There's nothing like homemade cassava bread. We make them quite flat similar to roti, but in St Lucia they are made in various thicknesses and can be combined with other ingredients to produce unique flavours.

2 lbs Cassava, peeled
1 tsp salt
1/2 tsp pepper

Method:
1. Peel and grate cassava.
2. Place in food processor and grate or use a hand grater.
3. Place grated cassava in clean tea towel and extract all liquid.
4. Put the grated cassava into a bowl, add salt and pepper and mix well.
5. Divide cassava into 4 portions.
6. Place a non stick frying pan on a medium heat until hot.
7. Put 1st portion of cassava into pan, spread evenly to form a circle to cover the base of pan.
8. Press cassava to base while cooking ensuring there are no gaps as bread cooks for about 3minutes or until golden brown.
9. Turn bread over and continue to cook till golden brown.
10. Remove from frying pan and place on grease proof paper to cool
11. Continue the process until the portions of cassava is cooked.

monica's cornbread

Cornbread is traditionally thought of as an American dish, but corn is readily available across the Caribbean and we've made this bread many times for family parties and BBQ's. It's delicious, try it!

1 1/2 cups corn meal
1 cup plain flour
300 mls milk
150g butter, melted
100g caster sugar
3 large eggs, beaten
1tsp salt
2tsp baking powder

1/2 tsp bicarbonate of soda
zest and juice of 1 lemon
Vegetable oil for roasting tin
9" square baking/roasting tin

Method:

1. Preheat oven to gas mark 7.
2. Grease roasting tin/tray with vegetable and place in oven to keep hot while the batter is prepared.
3. In a mixing bowl place the corn meal, plain flour, sugar, baking powder bicarbonate of soda, lemon zest and salt and mix well.
4. Next add all the wet ingredients - milk, melted butter and lemon juice.
5. Mix well to form a smooth batter. Remove roasting tin from oven and pour in batter. Return to oven, bake for 35 to 40 minutes until golden brown.
6. Bread is done when a skewer is inserted and it comes out clean.
7. Leave in tin to cool slightly before turning out. Serve warm.

pumpkin muffins
makes 12

We love pumpkin in our family and what better way to enjoy this delightful vegetable in a tasty muffin! Tastes great with your favourite jam or with a slice of cheese.

2 cups plain flour2 tsp baking powder
1/2 tsp bicarbonate of soda
150g softened butter
3 large eggs, beaten
2 cups pumpkin puree
11/2 cups soft light brown sugar
2 tsp ground cinnamon
1tsp ground ginger
1/2 tsp ground allspice
1/4 tsp grated nutmeg

1/2 tsp salt
2 tsp vanilla extract
2 muffin trays - each tray does 6 muffins making 12 muffins in total
butter to grease tins
flour to dust tins to prevent sticking
Or 12 muffin cases

Method:
1. Preheat oven to gas mark 5.
2. In a mixing bowl, place sugar and butter, cream together to fluffy consistency.
3. Add beaten egg a little at a time and blend into butter sugar mixture.
4. Add vanilla extract and mix.
5. Add pureed pumpkin and mix well.
6. In another mixing bowl sift all the dry ingredients together.
7. Fold in the sifted dry ingredients into the wet mixture until all are blended together without over working it.
8. Divide batter into 12 equal portion into muffin cases.
9. Place in oven and bake on gas mark 5 for 25 - 30 minutes.
10. Muffins are cooked when skewer inserted, it comes out clean.
11. Leave to cool slightly in muffin trays before turning out onto a wire rack.

1 pot dinners

callaloo & crab soup

Callaloo is a green vegetable similar to spinach and tastes superb in soups. This soup can be eaten as a starter or as a main meal. You can substitute the crab for any fish of your choice.

Main Ingredients:
200g spinach
1 large Tin callaloo drained
2 cloves garlic minced
1 medium onion minced
1 scotch bonnet pepper, deseeded and minced
3 tsp fresh thyme leaves
1 litre vegetable stock
1 tsp sea salt
1/2 tsp black pepper
2 Tbs olive oil
200g cooked crab
200 mls coconut milk

Vegetables:
1 cup diced carrots
1 cup diced potatoes
1 cup diced green bananas

Dumplings:
1cup plain flour
1/2 tsp baking powder
1/2 tsp sea salt
1/4 tsp black pepper
1 tsp sugar
25g butter
warm water

Dumpling Method:
1. In mixing bowl place all ingredients and combine.
2. Add water a little at a time until a firm dough is formed.
3. Cover until needed.

Soup Method:
1. Place large saucepan on heat, add olive oil and minced onion, saute' for about 5 minutes until soft and slightly golden.
2. Add minced garlic, scotch bonnet pepper and fresh thyme leaves and saute' for a further 1 minute.
3. Add spinach and wilt down.
4. Add drained callaloo and cook for 2 minutes.
5. Add vegetable stock and bring to the boil and simmer for 10 minutes.
6. Remove saucepan from heat, using hand held blender blitz soup.
7. Return saucepan to heat and add chopped vegetables and bring to boil.
8. Add dumplings and bring to the boil .
9. Reduce heat and simmer for 15 minutes until vegetables and dumpling are cooked.
10. Add coconut milk and crab and bring back to boiling point until crab is heated through.
11. Adjust seasoning.
12. Remove from heat and serve.

roasted butternut squash & coconut soup serves 4-6

Butternut squash is one of our favourite vegetables! It's very healthy and teamed with coconut it makes a delicious soup for cosy winter evenings. Enjoy!

Ingredients:

2kg butternut squash, peeled and cut into 2" cubes
1 medium onion, chopped
2 cloves garlic chopped
400 mls coconut milk, reduced fat - optional

2 tbs chopped coriander
1 tbs olive oil
1 tsp sea salt
1/2 tsp black pepper
1 litre vegetable stock
1 tsp Tan Rosie's Garlic & Pepper Sauce (HOT)

Soup Method:

1. Preheat oven to gas mark 7.
2. Place butternut squash, onions, garlic, sea salt, pepper and olive oil in a roasting tray.
3. Mix well together to allow all ingredients to be covered with oil.
4. Roast for 40 minutes or until soft.
5. Place roasted vegetables and other ingredients in food blender and blitz until smooth.
6. Place blended mixture in saucepan, bring slowly to the boil, adjust seasoning
7. Serve in warmed bowls.

oxtail soup

Oxtail soup is a classic dish which is eaten throughout the Caribbean. It's perfect for those cold evenings when you want to eat a warming and comforting meal.

Dumpling Ingredients:
1 cup self raising flour
1/2 tsp sea salt
1/4 tsp black pepper

1 tsp sugar
25g butter
water to mix

Dumpling Method:
1. In mixing bowl, combine all dry ingredients, add enough water to make a firm dough. leave to rest.
2. Divide dough into 12 small balls
3. Leave until required

Soup Ingredients:
1 kg oxtail, fat trimmed off
1 large onion, chopped
2 carrots, chopped
2 stalks celery, chopped
2 cloves garlic, minced
2" piece fresh ginger, minced
1 tbs Tan Rosie's Jerk Rub
1 tbs Tan Rosie's Garlic & Pepper
Sauce (HOT) (optional)
1 tsp sea salt
1 tsp ground black pepper
2 to 3 tsp fresh thyme leaves
1 scotch bonnet pepper,
deseeded, chopped

2 Tbs barley
2 bay leaves
2 litres beef or vegetable stock
Vegetables:
150g diced carrots
150g diced potatoes
150g diced yams
150g diced pumpkin
300g cooked kidney beans

Soup Method:
1. Season oxtail with jerk seasoning, sea salt and pepper, cover and leave overnight in fridge.
2. Place large saucepan on heat source, add olive oil, onions, chopped carrots, celery, garlic and ginger, scotch bonnet peppers and thyme, saute' for 5 minutes.
3. Add oxtail to pan and saute' for a further 10 minutes
4. Add bay leaves, barley and stock to pan, bring to boil, cover saucepan, turn heat down and allow to simmer for 2 hours until oxtail is tender.
5. Sauce pan can be placed in oven on a medium heat - gas mark 6 - for 2 hours.
6. After 2 hours, add dumplings, and vegetables and continue to simmer in oven for a further 45 minutes.
7. Adjust seasoning to taste, remove from heat/oven and serve while hot.

traditional mutton soup

serves 4

We love mutton soup! It's an easy recipe to follow that has been made by our family for generations. You can substitute any vegetable of your choosing to suit your taste and you can also make this dish in a slow cooker.

Dumpling Ingredients:
1 cup self raising flour
1/2 tsp sea salt
1/4 tsp black pepper

1 tsp sugar
25g butter
water to mix

Dumpling Method:
1. In mixing bowl, combine all dry ingredients, add enough water to make a firm dough. Leave to rest.
2. Divide dough into 12 small balls .
3. Leave until required.

Soup Ingredients:
500g mutton on the bone, cut into 2" cubes
1 large onion, diced
2 carrots, diced
2 stalks celery, diced
2 cloves of garlic, minced
2" piece fresh ginger, minced
1 scotch bonnet pepper, deseeded and minced
2 tsp fresh thyme leaves
2 Tbs Tan Rosie Jerk Rub or an all purpose seasoning

1 Tbs Tan Rosie's Garlic & Pepper Sauce (HOT) (optional)
1 tsp sea salt
1 tsp ground black pepper
2 Tbs olive oil
2 bay leaves
100g pearl barley
2 litres beef or vegetable stock
150g diced potatoes
150g yams
150g green banana

Soup Method:
1. Season mutton, in a bowl, place mutton, jerk seasoning, sea salt, black pepper and hot sauce. Massage seasoning into meat, cover and leave in fridge over night.
2. Place large saucepan on to medium heat, add olive oil, onions, celery, carrots and saute' for 5 minutes until onions are translucent. Add ginger and garlic continue to saute'for a further 1 minute.
3. Add seasoned mutton to pan, cook for about 5 minutes. Add bay leaves, barley, thyme leaves and beef or vegetable stock. Bring to the boil, reduce heat, cover and simmer for 1 1/2 hours, stirring occasionally. Alternately, place covered saucepan into oven on gas mark 6 for 1 1/2 hours until mutton is tender.
4. Then remove from oven, add diced vegetables and dumplings. Return to oven and cook for a further 30 minutes.
5. After 30 minutes adjust seasoning and serve.

pigeon pea soup

This is a classic soup from our family home of Carriacou Grenada. It's eaten as a main meal in most households. Pigeon peas are a popular pulse and grow all over Grenada and Carriacou.

500g pigeon peas - Soaked in cold water overnight, then cooked in a change of water for 50 minutes until just soft but not overly so as would continue to cook when other ingredients are added.
Or 2 tins pigeons peas - already cooked
200g smokey bacon, cubed
1 large onion, chopped
2 cloves garlic, minced
2 tbs olive oil
2 sticks celery, diced
2 carrots, diced
2 tsp fresh thyme leaves
1/2 tsp ground black pepper
1/2 tsp ground allspice

1/4 tsp ground cloves
1 tsp sugar
1 scotch bonnet pepper, whole
1 tsp Tan Rosie Garlic and Pepper sauce (optional)
400 mls coconut milk
2 litres vegetable or chicken stock
100g potatoes, diced in 1" cubes
100g sweet potatoes, diced in 1" cubes
100g plantains, cubed
100g yams, cubed

For Dumplings:

150g plain flour
1/2 tsp salt
1/2 tsp sugar
20g butter
1/4 tsp ground black pepper
Water to mix a firm dough

Dumpling Method:

1. In a mixing bowl place all the dry ingredients and rub in the butter.
2. Add enough water to form a firm dough.
3. Cover and leave to rest until required.

Soup Method:

1. Place a large saucepan on a medium heat, add olive oil and heat up.
2. Add onion and saute for 5 minutes until soft and slightly golden.
3. Add bacon to pan and fry for a further 5 minutes.
4. Add minced garlic and cook for a minute without burning.
5. Next add celery, scotch bonnet pepper, carrots and thyme and stir.
6. Add ground cloves, allspice, black pepper stir for 2 minutes .
7. Add coconut milk, stock and pigeon peas and bring to the boil, reduce heat and simmer for 25 minutes.
8. Add root vegetables- potatoes and yams, cook for 5minutes.
9. Add sugar and hot sauce, stir through.
10. Make dumplings - form dough into small balls 1inch size - marble sized.
11. Add dumplings to pigeon peas, stir and bring back to boil and continue to simmer.
12. Cook for a further 15 minutes until vegetables and dumplings are cooked.
13. Remove scotch bonnet pepper and discard.
14. Adjust seasoning to taste.

Tip: For vegetarian option omit the bacon!

meat & poultry

Caribbean Lime Roast Chicken

Caribbean Lime Roast Chicken Rub is an easy-to-use tasty seasoning created using freshly ground herbs and spices. Just add fresh limes to this delicious spice blend, it's the perfect summer dish.

8 Chicken Thighs, skinned
1 Packet Tan Rosie Caribbean Lime Roast
Chicken Rub
Zest and Juice of 2 Limes
60 mls Olive Oil

Method:
1. In a small bowl place chicken rub, olive oil, juice and zest of lime and stir to a paste.
2. Rub paste into chicken thighs to cover completely, then place in a sealed container and marinade for 24 hours at least.
3. Preheat oven to gas mark 7 (220c).
4. Place chicken thighs on a roasting tray and cover with foil then bake in oven for 45 minutes.
5. Remove foil covering and continue baking for a further 15 minutes.
6. Remove chicken from roasting tray to serving dish, cover to rest.
7. Place roasting tray on heat and reduce tray juices to a syrupy consistency.
8. Spoon reduced tray juice over chicken and serve.

Serving suggestion:
1. With a tossed salad and sweet potato chips.
2. With a cous cous salad.

jerk bbq ribs with sweet chilli & lime glaze serves 6

Prepare to be licking your fingers with this amazing jerk bbq ribs. They fall off the bone and taste superb in the sweet chilli and lime glaze. Delicious finger food for BBQ parties for all the family.

1 kg Pork ribs
2 tbs olive oil
1 tbs Tan Rosie's Jerk Rub
2 tsp veg stock powder or 1 stock cube crushed
200 mls Sweet chilli and lime The Sauce

Sweet Chilli & Lime Sauce Ingredients:
6 red chillies, chopped
3 limes, juice and zest of
1 cup granulated sugar
1/2 cup water
1/2 cup rice wine vinegar

Sauce Method:

1. In a saucepan add all the ingredients and place saucepan on a medium heat. Stir continuously until sugar has dissolved.
2. Bring to the boil and reduce heat to a simmer. Cook for 10 minutes then remove pan from heat and allow to cool slightly.
3. Pour into a sterilised bottle and cover and store in fridge until ready to use.

BBQ Ribs Method:

1. Place ribs in a bowl with a lid if possible. In another bowl, place the olive oil, stock, and jerk rub, mix well. massage mixture into ribs, cover and leave to marinade for 24 hours.
2. Preheat oven to gas mark 7.
3. Arrange ribs into a roasting tin, cover with foil and roast for 11/4 hours.
4. Then remove foil and brush on the sweet chilli and lime sauce and return to oven for a further 30 minutes, turning once.
5. Remove ribs from roasting tin and arrange on a serving platter.
6. Reduce down the pan juices from the ribs to a thickish consistency,
7. Soon over ribs and serve.

Tip: For a smooth sauce, blend until all chillies are completely dissolved.

Pollo Guisado

Pollo Guisado is a traditional dish from the Spanish Caribbean island Dominican Republic. It's a delicious hearty chicken stew made from a their traditional Sofrito base seasoning. Sofrito is a specific blend of sweet peppers, onions, garlic and herbs which is used in many dishes on this Spanish speaking island. Green olives are a direct influence from Spain which adds a special dimension to the dish.

Sofrito ingredients & method

2 green peppers, deseeded and chopped
1 red pepper, deseeded and chopped
1 yellow pepper, deseeded and chopped
2 red chillies, deseeded and chopped
2 green chillies, deseeded and chopped

4 medium sized plum tomatoes, chopped
4 medium onions chopped
3 heads of garlic, peeled
1 bunch coriander, roughly chopped
1/2 bunch flat leaf parsley, roughly chopped
1 tbs sea salt
1tbs ground black pepper

Method:
1. Place all ingredients into a food processor and blend together.
2. Next place into sterilised jar and store in refridgerator until ready to use.

Tips:
1: Sofrito can be used in stews, to cook rice.
2: Can be portioned into freezer bags and store in freezer until required.

Pollo Guisado ingredients & method

1kg Boneless, Skinless Chicken thighs cut into 2 cubes
1 large onion, minced
2 carrots, diced
2 sticks celery, diced
500g potatoes, diced
1 tin chopped tomatoes, or 1 cup homemade tomato sauce
1 tbs olive oil
1tbs sugar
1 cup sofrito, see recipe above

1 tbs garlic and ginger paste - 4 cloves garlic crushed with 2 inch piece ginger root
1 tsp sea salt
1tsp ground black pepper
1 tbs basil chopped
1 tbs chopped thyme
1cup olives
1/4 cup capers (optional)
2 cups chicken stock
1 scotch bonnet pepper, left whole

Method:
1. Preheat oven to gas mark 7.
2. In a mixing bowl place cut chicken, garlic and ginger paste, sea salt and black

pepper. Mix well into chicken and allow to marinade for 2 hours or over night.

3. On the hob, place a oven proof saucepan on medium heat.

4. Add olive oil and sugar and bring to a medium caramel colour.

5. Add chicken pieces to the caramelised sugar and stir to give chicken a light brown colour. Keep stirring continuously until all the chicken has a good colour.

6. Add onions to chicken and cook until onions are tender, this could be about 5 minutes.

7. Add carrots, celery, potatoes and sofrito to chicken and onions and continue to cook for 5 minutes.

8. Next, add thyme, basil, tomato sauce or tinned tomatoes, chicken stock and scotch bonnet pepper to pot.

9. Add olives and capers and stir.

10. Cover pot and place in oven and cook in a moderate oven on gas mark 7 for 50 minutes.

11. After 50 minutes remove from oven and return to hob.

12. Remove scotch bonnet pepper and discard.

13. Check seasoning, may need to add salt and pepper to taste

dominican republic beef kipes

Kipes or Quipes (pronounced: Kippays) is a traditional dish made with bulgar wheat from the Spanish speaking island of Dominican Republic. We think they are best served hot with a dip or sauce of your choice, rice and a fresh salad.

Casing: 2 cups Bulgar wheat
3 cups water
250g lean mince beef
1tsp sea salt
1/2 tsp ground black pepper

Kipes mix: 500g mince beef
2 large onions, minced
100g tomatoes, chopped
2tsp fresh thyme leaves
2 garlic cloves, minced

Filling:
1tbs grated ginger
1 scotch bonnet pepper, deseeded and minced
2tbs olive oil
1tbs Tan Rosie hot sauce -optional
2tsp ground allspice
1tsp sea salt
1tsp ground black pepper
100ml vegetable stock
1tbs Worcestershire sauce
vegetable Oil for deep Frying

Filling Method:
1. Place olive oil in a saucepan on medium heat, add onions and soften for 5 minutes until lightly golden.
2. Add garlic, ginger, allspice, thyme, scotch bonnet peppers,cook for 2 minutes.
3. Add mince beef, brown for 5minutes.
4. Add tomato to pan and continue cooking while stirring occasionally.
5. Add Worcestershire sauce, vegetable stock and black pepper and hot sauce, stir and continue cooking until all liquid has evaporated.
6. Remove from heat and leave to cool.

Casing Method:
1. Place bulgar wheat and water in a bowl and soak for 30 minutes.
2. Drain all the water from bulgar wheat and return to bowl.
3. Add mince beef, salt and pepper and mix well.
4. Transfer mixture to a food processor and blend to fine consistency.

To Make Kipes:
1. Take a handful of the bulgar wheat mixture, form a pocket and insert the mince beef filling and enclose to form torpedo shaped patties.
2. Continue making these patties until all filling and bulgar mixture is used up.
3. Place on a tray and rest in fridge for 30 minutes until firm.
4. Deep fry in batches until golden brown for 5 to 8 minutes.
5. Place on tray with kitchen paper on removal from fryer.

jamaican beef patties

Homemade patties are so much better than shop bought. You will taste the difference with these juicy meat filled delights. Lovely buttery pastry and a scrumptious beef curry filling, a real taste of Jamaica.

Pastry Ingredients:
21/2 cups plain flour
250g butter, cold
1 tsp salt
1 tsp turmeric
3/4 iced water

Method:

1. In a mixing bowl, place flour salt and turmeric and mix through. Grate the butter into the flour and mix through.

2. Add iced water a little at a time and bring all ingredients into a firm dough.

3. Turn dough out onto a floured surface and knead for one minute.

4. Wrap pastry in cling film and refridgerate for about 30 minutes at least or until ready for use.

Filling Ingredients:
500g minced beef
1 medium onion, chopped
2 cloves garlic, minced
2" piece root ginger, grated
2 tsp fresh thyme leaves
1 scotch bonnet pepper, deseeded and minced
1 cup diced carrots
1/2 cup diced celery
1 cup diced potato
1/2 cup beef stock or vegetable
1tbs Worcestershire sauce
1tbs Tan Rosie's Garlic & Pepper Sauce (HOT)
1tsp ground allspice
1/2 tsp ground cloves
1 tbs Tan Rosie Caribbean Style Curry Powder
1tsp sea salt
1/2 tsp ground black pepper
1tbs olive oil
1/2 cup bread crumbs

Filling Method:

1. Preheat oven to gas mark 7.

2. Need to use an oven safe saucepan with a lid.

3. Place saucepan on a medium heat source, add olive oil, onion, carrots, celery and scotch bonnet pepper, Saute' for 10 minutes until softened. Add garlic, ginger and thyme and continue cooking for a further 1 minute. Set aside

4. Add minced beef to same pan, and brown meat, stirring occasionally, for 10 minutes

5. Return onion mixture to pan with browned minced beef, add curry powder, allspice, ground cloves and black pepper, stir and cook for 2 minutes.

6. Add diced potato, beef stock, Worcestershire sauce, hot sauce and salt to taste, stir.

7. Cover with lid and place in oven to cook for 30 minutes.

8. Remove from oven, add bread crumbs and stir through, set aside to cool before use.

To Make Patties:
1. Preheat oven to gas mark 7.
2. Roll out pastry to a thickness of 1/8 inch thick.
3. Using a saucer cut out circles of pastry.
4. Place a heaped dessert spoonful of filling into centre of pastry disc. Moisten edges of pastry with water and fold over to seal.
5. With the tine of a fork, crimp edges to further seal and create a pattern.
6. Prick top of patties with fork to allow steam to escape during the baking process.
7. Place some parchment paper in baking tray before placing patties on tray.
8. Brush top with an egg wash - 1 egg beaten with 1 tbs water.
9. Continue filling all pastry discs as before until all pastry is used up.
10. Bake for 30 to 35 minutes until golden brown.

monica's bbq jerk chicken

serves 4

If you haven't tried our yummy jerk rub, then this is your chance. It's so easy to prepare and tastes delicious. It's mild to medium heat, so you can always add your own extra chilli.

4 Chicken pieces or 1 whole chicken
60mls Olive Oil
1 packet of Tan Rosie's Jerk Rub

Method:
1. Place 4 pieces of chicken/pork (or 1 whole chicken) into a bowl and rub with olive oil.
2. Massage 1 packet of Tan Rosie's Jerk Rub into chicken/pork & leave to marinade for 2 hours or preferably overnight in the fridge.
3. BBQ for 40mins or until cooked on medium heat.

That's it, easy!

caribbean beef stew

Stews are always very popular at our monthly pop-up supper club restaurant. You will enjoy trying this rich and tasty beef stew which goes very well with coconut rice (see side dishes chapter).

750g braising steak, cut in 2" cubes	1tbs olive oil
2 tbs vegetable oil	1 large onion, chopped
1 tbs sugar	2 carrots, diced
2 cloves garlic, minced	2 celery stalks, diced
2" root ginger, minced	200g diced potatoes
1 tsp ground allspice	1 tbs tomato puree
1 tsp ground black pepper	1 scotch bonnet pepper, whole
1/2 tsp ground cloves	2 tsp fresh thyme leaves
1 tbs Worcestershire sauce	2 cups beef or vegetable stock
1 tbs dark soya sauce	

1 tsp Tan Rosie's Garlic and Pepper Sauce (HOT)

Filling Method:

1. In a glass/pyrex type bowl, put cubed beef, add garlic, ginger, allspice, black pepper, Worcestershire sauce, soya sauce, hot sauce, olive oil and sea salt and massage into beef.

2. Cover bowl with cling film and leave to marinade in fridge overnight.

3. Using a heavy base saucepan, add vegetable oil, place on hob on medium heat. Allow oil to get quite hot, add sugar and caramelise to brown colour and frothy.

4. Pour in the marinated beef and stir continuously to colour all the meats and to brown. Saute for 5minutes.

5. Add Onions, cook for 5minutes until softened.

6. Add carrots, celery, potatoes, tomato puree, thyme leaves and scotch bonnet pepper and stir.

7. Pour in beef stock, stir. Cover saucepan and place in oven at Gas mark 6 for 1 1/2 hours.

8. Remove saucepan from oven, discard scotch bonnet pepper.

9. Serve with white rice and a green salad or steamed vegetables.

spiced slow roast leg of mutton

makes 4-6

We love slow roasted mutton in our family. The spice mix is delicious and gives the mutton amazing flavour. Make sure it's falling off the bone when it's cooked!

Spice Mix Ingredients:
2 tbs Allspice berries
2 sticks Cinnamon
1 tbs cloves
4 bay leaves

2 tbs coriander seeds
1 tbs black peppercorns
2 star anise
1 tbs chilli flakes

Spice Mix Method:
Put all the above ingredients in a spice grinder and grind to a fine powder. Store in a sealed air tight container, until ready for use.

Main Ingredients:
1 shoulder of mutton
4 tbs olive oil
4 tbs spice mix
2 tsp sea salt
1 tbs Tan Rosie's Garlic & Pepper Sauce (HOT)
2 tsp fresh thyme leaves
2 tsp minced garlic

2 tsp minced ginger
1 large onion, sliced
2 carrots, sliced
2 sticks celery, sliced
3 to 4 sprigs thyme
2 cups vegetable or lamb stock-
Pinch of sea salt and black pepper

Marinade Method:
Combine olive oil, spice mix, sea salt, hot sauce, garlic, ginger and thyme leaves in a small mixing bowl to create a paste. Make a few slits in shoulder of mutton and massage paste well into meat. Marinade shoulder of mutton and keep in the fridge.

Cooking Method:
1. Preheat oven to gas mark 8.
2. Using a roasting tray lined with foil, place the sliced onions, celery, carrots, thyme in roasting tin, sprinkle with salt and pepper. Place the marinaded shoulder of mutton on the vegetables, add the stock and cover with foil.
3. Place the roasting tin in oven and roast on high heat for 30 minutes.
4. Turn down to gas mark 5 and roast slowly for 5 hours.
5. After 5 hours, remove foil and turn heat up to gas mark 7 and continue to cook/brown top of roast for another 30 minutes, occasionally basting with the pan juices.
6. When cooking is finished, remove from oven, place meat on a serving platter and cover with foil to rest.
7. The pan juices can be sieved and reduced down with a knob of butter and drizzle over the roasted shoulder

monica's fried chicken serves 6

Served up at many of our supper club nights, our fried chicken is a fool-proof recipe! It's got incredible flavour with lovely a crispy coating and succulent flesh to taste. Enjoy.

6 Chicken legs, divide each leg in 2
1/2 tsp sea salt1/2 tsp ground black pepper
2 tsp Tan Rosie's Garlic and Pepper Sauce (HOT)
1 tbs olive oil
150g plain flour
1/2 tsp sea salt
1/2 tsp ground black pepper
1 tsp smoked paprika
1/2 tsp dried thyme
Vegetable oil for frying

Filling Method:
1. Marinade chicken legs in a small bowl combine sea salt, black pepper, hot sauce and olive oil to form a paste.
2. Rub paste into chicken legs, cover and marinade in fridge for 4 hours or overnight.
3. Next day remove from fridge and bring to room temperature. Using a freezer bag, add flour, sea salt, ground black pepper, smoked paprika and dried thyme, seal bag and shake to blend all ingredients. A large bowl will work as well.
4. Place a frying pan on medium heat, add vegetable oil and heat. In the mean time add chicken to freezer bag with the four mixture, seal bag and shake well to coat all chicken pieces completely.
5. Carefully place chicken pieces in the hot oil keeping each piece separate. Cook for 5 minutes then turn chicken over, cook for a further 5 minutes to seal the chicken.
6. Cover frying pan and continue cooking chicken for 15 minutes.
7. Remove lid and continue cooking to form a crisp outer coating for 8 to 10 minutes.
8. Cover a plate with kitchen paper. Take chicken from frying pan and place on plate with kitchen paper.

Tip: At step 6, place on a baking tray and roast for 20 minutes on gas mark 7 then serve.

slow roast bbq belly pork

serves 6-8

Belly pork is one of the most delicious cuts of pork you can buy, full of flavour and succulent. We slow cooked the pork then finished it off on the bbq for extra flavour. It's fantastic.

2.5kg Belly pork, skin scored
2 tbs olive oil
1 pk Tan Rosie Caribbean Rub
2 tsp minced garlic
2 tsp grated ginger
2 carrots, sliced

2 sticks celery, sliced
1 large onion, sliced
4 sprigs thyme
1 head of garlic
1/2 tsp sea salt
1/2 tsp ground black pepper
1 litre chicken or vegetable stock

Method:

1. Marinade Belly pork: In a small dish pour olive oil, Caribbean Rub, ginger and garlic and combine to form a paste.
2. Place belly pork in a lidded container.
3. Rub the prepared spice paste on the underside and sides of the pork joint.
4. To the skin side, dry well and sprinkle with salt and pepper.
5. Cover and leave to marinade for at least 24 hours in the fridge.
6. Next day remove from fridge and bring to room temperature.
7. Preheat oven to Gas Mark 8in a roasting tray, place a layer of foil, spread out the carrots, celery, onions, garlic and thyme.
8. Lay the belly pork Skin side up on the vegetable base.
9. Pour in the stock, fold the foil up around the sides of the belly pork with the skin exposed.
10. Roast on high heat, gas mark 8, for 30 minutes, then turn heat down to gas mark 5 and cook slowly for 3 hours.
11. After 6 hours turn up the oven to gas mark 7 and continue roasting for a further 30 minutes to obtain a nice crisp pork crackling.
12. Remove from oven and place meat on a serving platter and cover with foil loosely.
13. Strain the pan juices and reduce down.
14. Pour the sauce over the pork pieces and place on a BBQ for a few minutes either side and serve. Delish!

fish dishes

pan fried red snapper with a citrus salad   serves 4

Classic red snapper is best cooked simply in our opinion. We've lightly pan fried the fish and served it with a delightful mixed citrus salad. It looks stunning on the plate and taste amazing too. Perfect as a starter or a light lunch meal.

Fish Ingredients:
4 fillets red snapper
2 tbs plain flour
2tbs fine cornmeal
1tsp sea salt
1tsp ground black pepper
2tbs vegetable oil for pan frying

Citrus Salad Ingredients:
1 blood red Grapefruit, peeled and segmented
1 orange, peeled and segmented
1 lemon, peeled and segmented
1tbs fresh parsley, finely chopped
1 tbs chives, finely chopped
1 red chilli, minced
1tbs olive oil
1tsp sea salt
1/2 tsp ground black pepper

Pan Fry Fish Method:
1. Place 2 slashes on skin of each snapper fillet.
2. Combine flour, cornmeal, sea salt and black pepper in a freezer bag or a plate.
3. Coat each fillet with flour mixture, shake to remove excess flour and set aside.
4. Place a frying pan on medium heat, add vegetable oil and bring to heat.
5. To the hot pan place the fillets of fish skin side down and hold in place for 1/2 a minute to prevent curling up of fillet.
6. Continue cooking until skin side is golden and crisp this should take about 2 to 3 minutes depending on thickness of fillet.
7. Turn fillet over and cook for 1 to 2 minutes.
8. Remove from heat and serve with the citrus salad.

Citrus Salad Method:
1. Combine all the salad ingredients in a bowl and toss together.
2. Serve with panfried red snapper.

Crab Fritters

Fritters are a great streetfood dish which can be made from a variety of ingredients. We've created a juicy crab meat version which has appeared in our supper club pop restaurant events. They're best served with a dip that's got a little heat!

1 1/2 cups self raising flour
2 cups crab meat cooked
1/2 cup minced spring onions
1 red chilli, minced
1 green chilli. minced
2 tsp Tan Rosie's Garlic and Pepper Sauce (HOT)
2 eggs, beaten
2 tsp fresh thyme leaves
1 1/2 tsp sea salt
1/2 tsp black pepper
Water to mix
Vegetable oil for frying

Method:

1. Place first 10 ingredients into a mixing bowl and combine lightly.
2. Add water a little at a time to combine all the ingredients into a batter of dropping consistency.
3. Cover and set aside for 10 to 15 minutes.
4. Place frying pan on stove, add vegetable oil and bring to heat.
5. When oil is hot drop spoonfuls of batter into pan and cook until lightly golden brown, turn and cook on other side until cooked through.
6. Remove from oil with slotted spoon and place on kitchen absorbant paper.
7. Continue process until remainder of crab fritters are cooked.

Tip:

For a dip for fritters blend 1/2 cup mayonnaise and 1/4 cup Tan Rosie's Garlic and Pepper Sauce and serve.

creole callaloo, spinach & prawn tart

serves 6

These delicious tarts are great way to combine your favourite ingredients for a yummy starter or lunch dish. Callaloo creates a Caribbean twist to this beautiful tart which has a delectable creamy parmesan sauce.

6 blind baked individual tart cases
12 cooked prawns, halved

For Callaloo & Spinach Puree:
1 tin Callaloo, drained
200g spinach
3 shallots, minced
3 cloves garlic, minced
1tbs ginger, minced
1 scotch bonnet pepper, deseeded and minced
2tsp fresh thyme leaves
200ml coconut milk
1tbs olive oil
50g butter
1 vegetable stock cube, crushed
1/2 tsp sea salt
1/2 tsp ground black pepper
1/2 tsp palm sugar

For Cream Sauce:
1tbs olive oil
3 shallots, minced
2 bay leaves
500ml white wine
500ml vegetable stock or fish stock
100g butter
150ml double cream
1 scotch bonnet pepper, left whole

For Topping:
1 cup freshly grated Parmesan cheese
6 cooked prawns

Method:

1. In a saucepan on medium heat, add butter and olive oil and melt.
2. Add shallots, garlic, ginger, scotch bonnet pepper and thyme leaves and saute' for 5 minutes without colouring.
3. Add drained callaloo and spinach, stir and cook for 2 minutes.
4. Add coconut milk and stock cube crumbled.
5. Continue cooking until liquid is reduced down.
6. Season to taste with sea salt, sugar and black pepper.
7. Remove from the heat.
8. Using an electric blender puree mixture and set aside. Keep warm.

For Sauce:

1. Place butter, olive oil and shallots in a saucepan on a medium heat, cook for 5 minutes until softened.
2. Add bay leaves, scotch bonnet pepper and white wine, cook until reduced to a third.
3. Add stock and continue to cook to reduce to a third.
4. Add double cream to pan bring back to the boil and simmer to allow mixture to thicken. this should take 3 to 4 minutes.
5. Check seasoning.

6. Remove scotch bonnet pepper and bay leaves and discard.
7. Puree sauce using an electric blender and set aside. Keep warm.

To Assemble Tarts:
1. Place tart cases on a baking tray.
2. Place a tablespoonful of callaloo/spinach puree into each case.
3. Divide the halved prawns and add to tarts.
4. Cover the prawns with creamy sauce.
5. Sprinkle parmesan cheese on top to cover sauce.
6. Place tray under grill and allow cheese to toast.
7. Remove from grill and add a prawn on each tart to decorate.

Tip: For a vegetarian version, simply leave out the prawns!

crispy salt fish balls

makes 24

This is an interesting way to use salt fish. We've used Japanese Panko bread to add an extra crisp outer coating to these salt fish balls. They taste divine. Just make sure you make enough for your guests, as they will disappear quickly!

250g salt cod, rehydrated, deboned and flaked

1 lemon

3 medium potatoes, cubed and cooked

2tbs olive oil

200g onion, minced

100g tomatoes, chopped

1 green pepper, deseeded and diced

1 red pepper, deseeded and diced

1 scotch bonnet pepper, deseeded and minced

2 cloves garlic, minced

2tsp fresh thyme leaves

1tbs flat leaf parsley, finely chopped

2tbs Tan Rosie's Garlic & Pepper Sauce (HOT) - optional

1tbs fish sauce (optional)

1tsp sea salt

1/2tsp ground black pepper

vegetable oil for deep frying

Method:

1. Place salted cod in a lidded container with the juice of lemon and enough cold water to completely cover fish, leave to soak overnight or 24 hours. Change the water at least twice in this time period.

2. After 24 hours discard final water and cover with boiling water and leave to continue soaking for 2 hours. This allows all the saltiness to be removed and fish to flake easily.

3. Place the flaked fish in a mixing bowl, add boiled potatoes and mash together.

4. In a saucepan on medium heat, add olive oil and onions and saute' for 5 minutes, add garlic, peppers, thyme , cook for a further 5 minutes.

5. Remove from heat, add other ingredients and place in a food processor and coarsely blend.

6. Add to salt fish and potato mixture and mix thoroughly.

7. Leave mixture in fridge to firm up.

8. Next, divide mixture into 24 balls.

Coating Ingredients:

2 cups Panko bread crumbs

1 cup plain flour, seasoned with a pinch of sea salt and black pepper

2 to 3 eggs, beaten.

Tips:
1. Tinned salted cod can be used if available.
2. A potato ricer can be used to obtain a smoother mashed potato.

Coating Method:

1. Place the coating ingredients in 3 separate containers.

2. Coat fish balls in flour, then in beaten egg and finally coating in panko bread crumbs.

3. Place a piece of foil or parchment paper on a baking tray and place each coated ball to rest. Continue this process until all salt fish balls are completely coated.

4. Leave to rest for a further 30 minutes in fridge before deep frying.

5. Deep fry until golden brown.

6. Remove from fryer and onto a tray covered with kitchen paper.

100 fish dishes

trini prawn curry

Trini's love a good curry. Trinidad & Tobago cuisine has a strong Indian influence and they create some of the most tastiest curries. You will love eating this dish and your guests will want seconds!

Spice and Herb Paste:

2" fresh root ginger, grated
6 cloves garlic, minced
1 medium onion, chopped
1 red bell pepper, chopped
1 scotch bonnet pepper, deseeded
and chopped
2 tbs coriander, chopped

1 tsp fresh thyme leaves
2 tbs parsley, chopped
1 stick celery, stopped
4 spring onions, chopped
2 tbs white wine vinegar
1 tsp ground black pepper

Method:

Using a food processor, combine all the above ingredients and blend together to a fine paste.

500g raw prawns
**40g (2 pks) Tan Rosie Caribbean
Style Curry Powder**
2 tbs light olive oil
2 spring onions, chopped
1 small chilli pepper, chopped
1 tbs coriander chopped

Curry Method:

1. In a mixing bowl place the prawns, add 2 tbs of the spice and herb paste and toss together. Leave to marinade for 5 minutes.
2. Place a saucepan on medium heat, add olive oil and curry powder, stir, cook for 2 minutes on low heat to allow curry powder to cook without burning.
3. Add the marinaded prawns to curry and stir to incorporate all the ingredients. Cook for 3 to 4 minutes until prawn are pink and cook through.
4. Toss in spring onions, chopped chill and coriander and stir.
5. Serve boiled white rice or Trini 'Buss up Shut' Roti.

Tip: Left over spice and herb paste can be stored in fridge for up to 7 days or portioned out and freeze for up to 3 months!

ackee & saltfish tart

serves 6

This little twist on the classic Jamaican ackee & salt fish dish is fun, delicious and perfect for the summer. It's so easy to make and even quicker to eat!

250g salt Cod - re hydrated and deboned or 2 tins salt cod
1 lemon
150g onions, chopped
2 tbs olive oil
1 tsp garlic and ginger puree
1/2 green bell pepper, diced
1/2 yellow bell pepper, diced
1/2 red bell pepper, diced

15 mls fish sauce (optional)
280g tinned ackee, drained
1pk all butter puff pastry (1 sheet)
1/2 red chilli, diced
1/2 green chilli pepper, diced
1 tsp fresh thyme leaves
1/2 tsp ground black pepper
1 tsp Tan Rosie's Garlic and Pepper sauce (HOT)

Method:

How to prepare the salt cod: Place salt cod in a lidded container, add cold water and leave to soak with the sliced lemon, change the water a couple of times then leave to soak overnight. After 24 hours, discard that water and add boiled water to the salt cod and leave to soak or until water is cooled. Remove cod from water and discard the bones and skin from cod and flake the flesh and save.

1. Place a saucepan onto medium heat, add olive oil and onions and saute for 10 minutes on medium heat until onions have softened and golden brown.
2. Next peppers, chillies, thyme leaves and garlic and ginger puree and continue cooking for about 5minutes to soften peppers.
3. Add flaked salt cod, stir and continue cooking. Season mixture by adding ground black pepper, hot sauce and fish sauce, stir.
4. Add the drained ackee and gently fold into mixture and warm through, ackee just needs to bring to heat.
5. Remove salt cod and ackee mixture from heat and leave to cool before adding to pastry filling.
6. Preheat oven to gas mark 7.
7. Line baking tray with baking parchment.
8. Roll out puff pastry, divide into 6 equal squares.
9. Create a 1/2 inch border by lightly marking all the way round.
10. Divide filling into 6 and fill pastry sheets.
11. Brush outer border with egg wash.
12. Bake in oven for 25 minutes or until golden brown.
13. Serve with a nice salad.

vegetarian dishes

roasted pumpkin tart with feta cheese

makes 6-8

Pumpkins can be used in a wide variety of dishes. We served these perfectly formed tarts for a vegetarian starter at our supper club. They went down a storm and they're so easy to make too.

2 pks Ready made Puff pastry
500g pumpkin, diced
1 tbs olive oil
150g feta cheese, crushed
3 eggs, beaten
1/2 cup milk
1/2 cup double cream
2 tsp Tan Rosie's Garlic and Pepper Sauce (HOT)
1/2 tsp grated nutmeg
1/2 tsp sea salt
1/4 tsp ground black pepper
1/4 cup grated parmesan cheese

Method:

1. Preheat oven to Gas mark 6.
2. Roll out pastry, cut into 6 5" discs to fit into muffin tins.
3. Fit pastry discs into muffin tins and blind bake for 15 minutes using baking beans.
4. Remove baking beans and return pastry to oven for a further 5 minutes to allow the base to dry out.
6. Remove from oven and set aside to cool.
7. In a baking tray place pumpkin and olive oil and roast for 20 to 30 minutes.
8. Set aside to cool. Prepare the custard, in a mixing jug place milk, double cream, garlic and pepper sauce, grated nutmeg, beaten eggs, salt and pepper and whisk well.
9. Divide roasted pumpkin and feta cheese into the pastry cases.
10. Pour custard over pumpkin and feta, sprinkle over with the parmesan cheese.
11. Bake in oven on gas mark 5 for 35 minutes until custard is set and parmesan is lightly golden.

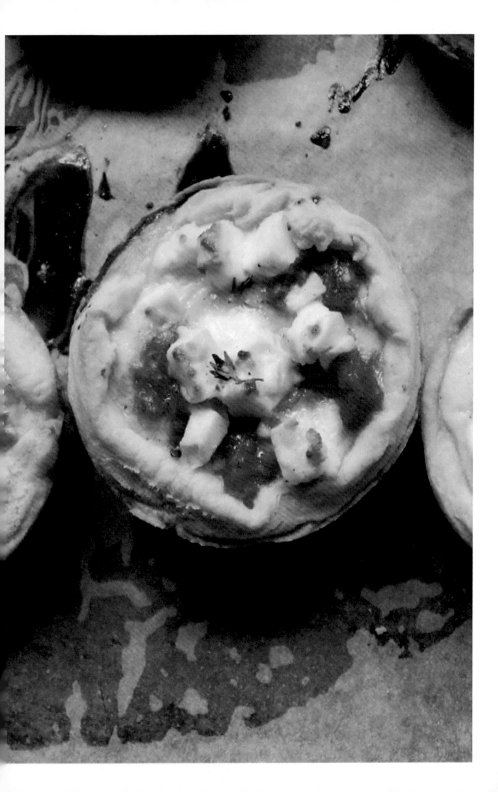

veggie curry patties

makes 16

This is a superb veggie alternative curry pattie recipe. Lovely as a snack or starter dish for the whole family.

Rough puff pastry - see recipe on page 78
2 tbs olive oil
200g potatoes, diced
150g carrots, diced
100g onions, chopped
2 cloves garlic, minced
1tbs grated ginger
100g frozen peas
2tsp fresh thyme leaves

2tbs Tan Rosie Caribbean style Curry Powder
1 scotch bonnet pepper, deseeded and minced
200ml vegetable stock
1 cup bread crumbs
1/2 tsp sea salt
1/2 tsp ground black pepper
1 egg, beaten for glazing

Filling Method:

1. On a medium heat, place a saucepan, add olive oil and onions, fry for 5 minutes until softened and lightly golden brown.
2. Add garlic, ginger, thyme leaves and scotch bonnet peppers, fry for a further 1 minute.
3. Add curry powder, continue to fry stirring to prevent burning for 1 minute.
4. Add diced potatoes, carrots and vegetable stock and bring to the boil. Place lid on saucepan and reduce heat and simmer for about 10 minutes until vegetables are tender.
5. Remove lid and continue cooking to allow all liquid to evaporate.
6. Take off the heat, add bread crumbs and season with sea salt and black pepper.
7. Set aside to cool before filling pastry.

To Make Patties:

1. Preheat oven to gas mark 7.
2. Roll out rough pastry to 1/8 inch thickness. Cut out 6 inch circles.
3. Place filling in centre, moisten edges with water, fold over to form a semi-circle. Crimp together to seal with the teeth of a fork.
4. Place patties on a greased baking tray.
5. Brush patties with beaten egg.
6. Prick top with a fork to allow steam out while cooking.
7. Continue until all circles are filled.
8. Bake in oven at gas mark 6 for 35 minutes or until golden brown.

aubergine & mushroom kipes

makes 10

Kipes or Quipes (pronounced: Kippays) is a traditional dish made with bulgar wheat from the Spanish speaking island of Dominican Republic. We think they are best served hot with a dip or sauce of your choice, rice and a fresh salad.

Casing Ingredients:

2 cups Bulgar wheat

3 cups water

250g mushrooms chopped

1 aubergine, chopped

1tsp sea salt

1/2 tsp ground black pepper

Casing Method:

1. Place bulgar wheat and water in a bowl and soak for 30 minutes.
2. Drain all the water from bulgar wheat and return to bowl.
3. Add mushroom, aubergine, salt and pepper and mix well.
4. Transfer mixture to a food processor and blend to fine consistency.

Filling Ingredients:

250g mushrooms, chopped

1 large Aubergine, diced

100g tomatoes, chopped

2tsp fresh thyme leaves

2 garlic cloves, minced

1tbs grated ginger

1 scotch bonnet pepper, deseeded and minced

2tbs olive oil

1tbs Tan Rosie's Garlic & Pepper Sauce (HOT) -optional

1tsp ground allspice

1tsp sea salt

1tsp ground black pepper

100ml vegetable stock

1tbs Worcestershire sauce

1tbs Mushroom ketchup - optional

vegetable Oil for deep Frying

Filling Method:

1. Place olive oil in a saucepan on medium heat, add onions and soften for 5 minutes until lightly golden.
2. Add garlic, ginger, allspice, thyme, scotch bonnet peppers, cook for 2 minutes.
3. Add mushrooms and cook for 5minutes.
4. Add aubergine to pan and continue cooking while stirring occasionally.
5. Add Worcestershire sauce, Mushroom ketchup, vegetable stock and black pepper and hot sauce, stir and continue cooking until all liquid has evaporated.
6. Remove from heat and leave to cool.

To Make Kipes:

1. Take a handful of the bulgar wheat mixture, form a pocket and insert the mushroom/aubergine filling and enclose to form torpedo shaped patties.
2. Continue making these patties until all filling and bulgar mixture is used up.
3. Place on a tray and rest in fridge for 30 minutes until firm.
4. Deep fry in batches until golden brown for 5 to 8 minutes.
5. Place on tray with kitchen paper on removal from fryer.

aubergine, sweet potato & spinach curry   serves 4-6

You will not miss meat with our succulent aubergine, sweet potato and spinach curry. It's so easy to make, filling and delicious. Serve with a fragrant chutney of your choice.

1 kg sweet potato, cut in 2" cubes
500g Baby aubergine, cut into 2" pieces
2 tbs olive oil, for roasting above vegetables
1 tsp salt
1/2 tsp black pepper
150g onions, chopped
2 cloves garlic, minced
1 whole scotch bonnet pepper
2 tsp fresh thyme leaves
2" piece fresh ginger, grated

40g (2 pks) Tan Rosie's Caribbean Style Curry Powder
1 tbs olive oil
1 tbs butter
400 ml coconut milk
400 ml vegetable stock
1 tsp sugar
salt and pepper to season
500g Spinach

Method:

1. Preheat oven to gas mark 6.

2. In a roasting tray, place sweet potato and aubergine, add salt and pepper and toss in the olive oil. Roast for 30 minutes.

3. On a medium heat, place a saucepan, add olive oil and butter and chopped onions. Cook onions for 5 minutes until golden brown. Add garlic and ginger and saute for a further 1 minute.

4. Add curry powder and fry for 1minute.

5. Add coconut milk, vegetable stock, thyme leaves, scotch bonnet pepper and sugar. Bring to the boil and simmer uncovered for 10 minutes to reduce down slightly.

6. Toss in roasted vegetables, continue to cook for a further 5 minutes. Add the spinach to pan and allow to wilt down.

7. Adjust seasoning with salt and pepper to taste. Remove scotch bonnet pepper and discard.

8. Serve with steamed basmati rice.

christophene & roasted pumpkin gratin   serves 4

This is a fabulous St Lucian vegetarian dish we ate at a family restaurant whilst on holiday. Christophene is a crisp and crunchy vegetable shaped like an avocado. This is an ideal dish to satisfy any meat eater or vegetarian!

Main Ingredients:

1 kg Pumpkin, peeled and cut into 1" cubes
1 christophene, peeled, deseeded and diced
1 medium onion, chopped
2 cloves garlic, minced
2 tsp fresh thyme leaves
2 tbs olive oil
1 tsp sea salt
1/2 tsp ground black pepper

Sauce Ingredients:

1 tbs plain flour
100g butter
450 mls milk
1 cup grated mature cheddar
1/2 cup grated parmesan cheese
1 tsp mustard powder
1/4 tsp grated nutmeg
1tbs Tan Rosie Garlic & Pepper Sauce (HOT)

Topping Ingredients:

1 cup bread crumbs
1/4 cup grated cheddar cheese
1/4 cup grated parmesan cheese
50g butter
1tsp fresh thyme leaves
pinch sea salt and black pepper

Method:

1. Preheat oven to gas mark 7.
2. In a baking tray place pumpkin, onions, garlic, fresh thyme leaves, sea salt and black pepper, add olive oil and toss so as all vegetables are coated. Roast for 40 minutes then set aside.
3. Place christophene in a saucepan of lightly salted water, bring to the boil and simmer for 10 minutes until tender. Remove from heat and drain.
4. Combine roasted pumpkin and parboiled christophene.

For Sauce:

1. Place saucepan on heat, add butter and allow to melt. Add flour, stir until butter absorbs all the flour. Add the milk a little at a time while stirring, a whisk is ideal to help in the incorporating process. A smooth consistency is the aim.
2. Continue stirring and allow to cook for 5 to 6 minutes on a simmer.
3. Remove pan from heat, Add cheeses, hot sauce, nutmeg, mustard powder and stir until cheese has melted into sauce. Check for seasoning, add a pinch of salt if required. Remember the cheeses are salty!
4. Grease an 9 inch pie dish with some butter.

5. Place a spoonful of sauce on base of pan, add a layer of pumpkin and christophene and top with a layer of sauce. Continue layering ending with a layer of sauce.
6. Combine breadcrumbs, cheddar and parmesan cheeses, butter thyme leaves salt and pepper to form a loose crumble.
7. Spread crumble over sauce.
8. Bake in oven for 40 minutes on gas mark 6.
Tip:
Butternut squash can be substituted for pumpkin.

stuffed spiced aubergines

This is a fantastic vegetarian main dish we've served up at our Supper Club. There are always clean plates when we clear up. Why would you need meat? Enjoy with a sauce of your choosing.

Ingredients for Stuffing:

500g mushrooms, chopped

2 tbs olive oil

1 cup cooked rice

1/2 yellow bell pepper, diced

1/2 green bell pepper, diced

1 red chilli, diced

1 medium onion, chopped

2 garlic cloves, minced

1 tsp grated root ginger

2 tsp fresh thyme leaves

1/2 tsp sea salt

1/2 tsp ground black pepper

1 tbs Worcestershire Sauce

1 tsp Tan Rosie Garlic and Pepper Sauce (HOT)

Cocktail sticks

Method:

1. Place a saucepan on to medium heat, add olive oil and onions and sauté for 5 minutes until softened and translucent, stirring occasionally.

2. Add mushrooms and continue to sauté, and mushrooms have released their liquid and its evaporated.

3. To mixture add peppers, chilli, garlic, ginger, thyme leaves and continue cooking and stirring for 5 minutes.

4. Add Worcestershire sauce, hot sauce and cooked rice and stir to combine.

5. Season with sea salt and black pepper.

6. Set aside to cool.

Aubergines:

3 large Aubergines, sliced length-wise in 1/2 inch thickness

3 tbs olive oil

Pinch sea salt

Pinch Black pepper

Method:

1. Place a griddle pan on a medium heat.

2. Brush each aubergine with olive oil and grill for 2 to 3 minutes on either side.

3. Put aside and continue cooking all the aubergines.

Method for Stuffing Aubergines:

1. Preheat oven to gas mark 6.

2. Line a baking tray with parchment paper.

3. Place 1 spoonful of the filling into the grilled aubergine, roll up to retain filling. Use cocktail stick to keep together and place on parchment paper.

4. Continue filling and folding the aubergines until all filling is used up.

5. Bake in oven for 20 to 25 minutes.

6. Serve with the jerk pepper sauce as a starter or a vegetarian main course.

Tip: Cooked bulgar wheat can replace the rice for the stuffing.

caramalised onion & callaloo patties — makes 10

You will be in vegetarian heaven with these amazing patties. Full of flavour and very filling. You can make them in advance for parties or lunch. We've served them as a starter dish, but can be eaten as a snack too.

Rough Puff Pastry:

225g plain flour

140g butter

1/2 tsp salt

90 - 140ml ice water

Method:
1. In mixing bowl, sift flour and salt.
2. Dice butter into half inch pieces and add to flour.
3. Cut butter into flour to coat.
4. Add water and mix to for a firm door without breaking up the too much.
5. Knead very lightly and form into a ball.
6. Wrap in cling film and leave to rest in refrigerator for at least 30 minutes.

Filling:

500g onions, sliced

2 tbs olive oil

30g butter

1 tsp garlic and ginger puree

75g spring onions

50g red and green chilli chopped

2 tsp fresh thyme leaves

400g tinned callaloo, drained

2 tsp sugar

1/2 tsp ground black pepper

1 tsp sea salt

1 tsp Tan Rosie Garlic and Pepper sauce (HOT)

125g fresh bread crumbs

Method:
1. Place saucepan on heat, add olive oil, onions and butter and saute on medium heat for about 15 minutes until softened and golden brown, stirring occasionally.
2. Add sugar and allow onions and sugar to caramelise and stir.
3. Add garlic and ginger puree, spring onions, red and green chillies and thyme, stir and continue to sauté for 5 minutes.
4. Stir in the drained Callaloo and stir.
5. Add hot sauce, salt and black pepper and season to taste.
6. Stir in bread crumbs and remove from heat.
7. Leave to cool before filling pastry.

Method to make Patties:
1. Preheat oven to gas mark 7. Cover baking tray with baking parchment, roll out rough puff pastry and cut out 6 inch discs.
2. Place 1 tablespoon of filling into centre of each pastry disc.
3. Brush edges with cold water. Fold over and crimp edges with the prongs of a fork.
4. Brush with egg wash and prick to allow steam out.
5. Arrange patties on baking tray and bake for 25 to 30 minutes on gas mark 7 until golden brown.
6. Remove from oven when cooked and cool on a wire rack.

spiced 3 bean stew & dumplings

Bean stews are very popular in the Caribbean especially with juicy dumplings. It's a hearty meal, very warming. Perfect for a Saturday afternoon lunch.

For Dumplings:

1 cup plain flour

1/2 tsp baking powder

1 tbs butter, melted

1 tsp sugar or honey

1/2 tsp sea salt

1/4 tsp ground black pepper

1 tbs chopped chives

1 tbs chopped parsley

Water to mix

Dumplings Method:

1. In a mixing bowl place all the ingredients except the water and combine together.

2. Add water to mix to a firm dough

3. Cover with cling film and set aside.

Ingredients for stew:

1 cup cooked Black beans

1 cup cooked kidney beans

1 cup cooked Black eye peas

400 mils coconut milk

400 mils vegetable stock

2 tbs olive oil

1 tbs butter

1 medium onion, chopped

2 tsp fresh thyme leaves

1 tbs grated fresh ginger

3 cloves garlic, minced

2 tsp Tan Rosie's Jerk Rub

1/4 tsp ground Allspice

1/4 tsp ground cloves

1 tsp ground black pepper

1/2 scotch Bonnet Pepper, deseeded and minced

1 tbs chopped parsley

1 tbs Worcestershire sauce

1 tsp Palm sugar or brown sugar

1 tsp sea salt

Method:

1. Place a sauce pan on medium heat, add olive oil, butter and onions, cook onions over low heat until softened to a light golden colour.

2. To this mixture add grated ginger, garlic and scotch bonnet pepper, stir and cook for one minute.

3. Add jerk seasoning, ground allspice, ground cloves, and black pepper, stir to prevent sticking to pan.

4. Stir in coconut milk, vegetable stock and thyme leaves, bring to the boil, reduce heat and simmer for ten minutes.

5. Add black beans, kidney beans and black eye peas cook for five minutes.

6. Stir in Worcestershire sauce and palm sugar.

7. Make the dumplings by rolling bits of the dough into one inch balls and adding to pan and stir.

8. Cover pan and cook on simmer for 10 minutes stirring occasionally.

9. Remove lid check the seasoning and adjust.

10. Stir in fresh parsley and serve.

vegetable lokri

serves 4-6

We've taken influence from a traditional Haitian recipe to create a delicious vegetarian rice dish. It's packed with flavour. Perfect as a quick lunch dish or you can eat this as a side dish for a main meal too.

2 cups Basmati rice
2 tbs olive oil
1 tbs butter
1 onion, chopped
2 carrots, diced
1 stalk celery, diced
1 red bell pepper, diced
1 yellow bell pepper, diced
1 red chilli, diced

2 tsp minced garlic
2 tsp grated ginger
2 tsp fresh thyme leaves
2 tbs parsley, chopped
4 spring onions, chopped
400ml coconut milk
400ml vegetable stock
1/2 tsp sea salt
1/4 tsp ground black pepper

Method:

1. Place a saucepan on medium heat, add olive oil, butter and onions, sauté and stir for 5 minutes until softened and lightly golden brown.

2. Add carrots, celery, peppers, chilli, garlic, ginger, thyme leaves and spring onions and stir, cook for 5 minutes.

3. Add rice and stir until all grains of rice is coated with the mixture.

4. Add coconut milk, vegetable stock, season with salt and pepper and bring to the boil.

5. Turn heat down to low to a gentle simmer for 13 minutes then turn off heat.

6. Stir through the chopped parsley while fluffing the rice.

7. Leave to rest for 5 to 10 minutes before serving.

side dishes

coo coo poi

Coo Coo Poi (polenta and peas) was a staple dish in our family home whilst growing up in Carriacou, Grenada. My grandma Tan Rosie, first cooked this for me when I was younger. It's great served with stewed meats with a rich sauce.

500g cooked pigeon peas or 2 tins
pigeon/gungo peas drained
2 tsp Tan Rosie's Jerk Rub
400 mls coconut milk
400 mls vegetable stock
1 medium onion, chopped
1 clove garlic, minced
2 tsp fresh thyme leaves
2 tbs olive oil
1 cup polenta or cornmeal

Method:

1. Place a saucepan on a medium heat, add oil and onion and saute for 5 minutes until translucent. Add garlic, stir and cook for a further 1 minute. Add thyme leaves, jerk rub, pigeon peas, coconut milk and stock, stir and bring to the boil. Reduce heat and simmer for 15 minutes.

2. Add polenta, stirring continuously to avoid forming any lumps. Extra water can be added if necessary to create a loose consistency.

3. Cook for 5 minutes. If using Cornmeal the cooking time will be much longer at around 30 minutes.

Tip: Quick cook polenta is ideal because it saves time!

deep fried okra

serves 4

This is a fantastic way to eat okra! We've created a lovely batter mix which is super crunchy and tasty complimenting the flavour of the okra. Perfect as a light snack with a touch of hot sauce!

500g okra, cut into 2" portions
3 cups vegetable oil for deep
frying
300mls buttermilk
2 tsp Tan Rosie Garlic & Pepper
Sauce (HOT)
1/2 cup fine cornmeal
1 cup plain flour
2 tsp Tan Rosie's Jerk Rub
1/2 tsp ground black pepper

Method:
1. In a mixing bowl pour buttermilk and hot sauce and mix well together. In another bowl pour cornmeal, flour, jerk seasoning and black pepper.
2. Using a whisk blend all these dry ingredients well. This will be the coating for the okra.
3. Place a wok or a dutch pot on the heat, add the vegetable oil bring to medium hot temperature.
4. The oil will be ready for frying by dropping small piece of bread in the oil if it sizzles and rise to top, it is ready for deep frying.
5. Dip each portion of okra in the buttermilk mixture and then into the flour mixture to coat okra completely.
6. Next lower the coated okra into the hot oil and fry/cook. The okra can be done in batches to avoid over crowding the pot.
7. Fry until golden brown, about 5 to 8 minutes.
8. Using a slotted spoon remove fried okra from oil and place on a plate with some kitchen paper to absorb excess oils.
9. Repeat process until all okra is fried.
10. Serve immediately while still hot!

pan fried plantains with a polenta crust

serves 4-6

Coating plantains in cornmeal is a super way to enjoy this popular Caribbean vegetable. The cornmeal coating adds a light crunch to the soft sweet ripe plantain. Delicious!

3 Ripe Plantains, peeled, divided into quarters
1/2 cup fine cornmeal
1tbs plain flour
1tsp sea salt
1/2 tsp ground black pepper
1 cup vegetable oil for frying

Method:
1. Combine cornmeal, plain flour, salt and pepper in a freezer bag and shake.
2. Place plantain pieces in the flour mixture and toss.
3. Remove plantains from bag and shake off excess coating.
4. Place on tray while oil is heating up.
5. Add vegetable oil to frying pan and bring to heat. Test the temperature is right by dropping a crumb of bread in the oil, when it sizzles its right for frying.
6. Place plantains in pan, fry until golden brown, turn and continue cooking until all is golden brown.
7. Remove with a slotted spoon and place on a try with kitchen paper to absorb excess oil.

Tips:
1. Serve as a side dish or even as part of a breakfast dish!
2. Great with BBQ dishes

jamaican style rice and peas

serves 4-6

Jamaican style rice & peas uses kidney beans. Many islands have their own take on this dish from using different beans (or peas) and spices. Of course, it's fantastic with curry mutton or jerk chicken!

2 cups cooked kidney beans
1 1/2 cups Long grain easy cook rice
400mls coconut milk
600mls vegetable stock
1 medium onion, chopped
2 garlic cloves, minced
2 tsp fresh thyme leaves
2 tbs olive oil
1 tbs butter
1 tsp Tan Rosie's Jerk Rub
1 tsp sea salt
1 tsp ground black pepper
1 whole scotch bonnet Pepper

2 tbs chopped coriander
1 tbs olive oil
1 tsp sea salt
1/2 tsp black pepper
1 litre vegetable stock
1 tsp Tan Rosie Garlic & Pepper Sauce (HOT)

Method:

1. Place a lidded saucepan on a medium heat on the hob.
2. Add olive oil and butter and allow to melt together.
3. Add chopped onions to pan and saute for 6 minutes until soften but not coloured.
4. Add minced garlic and saute for one minute.
5. Next add the fresh thyme leaves, Tan Rosie's jerk rub, stir to prevent sticking to pan.
6. Add Kidney beans, coconut milk and vegetable stock and bring to the boil. Stir in the long grain rice, season with sea salt and black pepper and scotch bonnet pepper and bring to the boil.
7. Check seasoning. Lower heat to a simmer, cover with a tight fitting lid and allow to cook so that all the liquid is absorbed, this should be 15 minutes.
8. Remove scotch bonnet pepper and discard.
9. After 15 minutes, remove from heat, fluff up rice and peas replace lid and leave for 10 minutes before serving.

crushed cassava & garlic mash

serves 4-6

This is a great alternative to regular mash potato. Cassava has a creamy consistency combined with garlic it's divine!

500g Cassava, peeled and cubed
1 tsp sea salt
1 litre water
4 cloves garlic, minced
2 tbs olive oil
2 tbs butter
1/2 tsp ground black pepper
1/2 tsp sea salt
1/2 cup double cream, warmed

Method:
1. Place saucepan on medium heat.
2. Add water and bring to the boil.
3. Add cassava to boiling water and cook for eight minutes or until cassava is cooked - if a skewer is put into cubes it gives way!
4. Drain water from cassava. Reserve the liquid.
5. Set aside the cassava in a covered bowl.
6. Replace saucepan on medium heat, add olive oil, butter and minced garlic, saute for one minute to cook being careful not to allow garlic to colour.
7. Add cooked cassava to pan mixed through the garlic and butter mix.
8. Using a potato masher, crush the cassava.
9. Stir in the warmed double cream and mix until well blended into cassava. Serve.

Tips:
1. Serve as a side dish instead of potatoes or rice.
2. Use as a topping for any pie dish, e.g. cottage pie.

callaloo fritters

makes 12-16

Callaloo is very similar to spinach and tastes scrumptious in these wonderful fritters. You can eat them as a quick snack or team with a green salad and salsa.

x1 450 tin callaloo, drained or
500g of wilted spinach
1 1/2 cups self raising flour
2 eggs beaten
4 spring onions, chopped
2 tsp fresh thyme, chopped
1/4 cup parsley chopped
2 green chillies, deseeded and
minced finely
1 tsp sea salt
1 tsp ground black pepper
**2 tsp Tan Rosie's Garlic & Pepper
Sauce (HOT)**
1tbs vegetable stock powder
Vegetable oil for frying

Method:

1. In a mixing bowl, combine all the ingredients all the ingredients except for the oil.
2. Mix to form a soft batter. Leave to rest in fridge for 1 hour.
3. Using a heavy bottomed saucepan, place vegetable oil in pan, bring to a medium heat.
4. Drop in spoonful of the mixture in pan, allow to cook until golden brown, turn to allow an all over goldenness.
5. This process may take up to 10 minutes depending on the size of the balls.
6. Remove from pan when cooked and place on a tray lined with kitchen paper to absorb excess oil.
7. Serve while still warm with a dip of your choice.

pumpkin cous cous

This is another fantastic way to use pumpkin. It's so easy to make when you are short of time. Tastes great for summer BBQ's, light lunches and more.

Main ingredients:
500g pumpkin, peeled and diced
1 medium red onion, chopped
1 red chilli, diced
2 tbs olive oil
1 tsp sea salt
1/2 tsp ground black pepper

For Cous Cous:
1 cup cous cous
1 cup vegetable stock, hot
1 tbs olive
2 tbs flat leaf parsley, finely chopped

Method:
1. Preheat oven to gas mark 7.
2. In baking tray combine all the main ingredients, and spread flat.
3. Bake in oven for 35 minutes stirring once half way through roasting process.
4. Place couscous in a bowl, add vegetable stock and olive oil, stir.
5. Cover bowl with cling film and leave until all liquid is absorbed into couscous, about 10 minutes.
6. Using a fork, fluff up the couscous, add the roasted pumpkin and chopped parsley and mix through.
7. Serve as a side dish with grilled fish or chicken.

Tip: Pumpkin can be replaced with butternut squash.

coconut & callaloo rice

serves 6-8

Coconut and callaloo are delightful combined in this yummy rice dish. We've served it with a Caribbean beef stew for a delicious evening meal.

2 cups basmati rice
250g chopped spinach or
1 tin Callaloo, drained
6 spring onion, chopped
2 tbs olive oil
400ml coconut milk
300ml vegetable stock
1/2 tsp sea salt
1/4 tsp ground black pepper

Method:

1. Wash basmati rice in 2 to 3 changes of water and leave to drain in sieve.
2. Place saucepan on heat and add olive oil, chopped spring onions. Soften spring onions without colouring it.
3. Add drained rice, stir so that all the rice grains are coated in the oil.
4. Add callaloo or spinach and allow it to wilt down while stirring.
5. Next add coconut milk, vegetable stock, salt and black pepper and stir.
6. Bring to the boil, reduce heat and simmer slowly for 10 to 12 minutes.
7. Turn heat off and leave cooked rice to rest for 5 minutes before fluffing up and serving.

salads

roasted sweetcorn and sweet pepper salad serves 4-6
with garlic & ginger

Corn is a staple vegetable in our family homeland of Carriacou in Grenada. Roast corn is a popular streetfood found on many islands around the Caribbean too. We've made this into a tasty summer salad which can accompany any main dish.

4 sweetcorn on the cob
1 red pepper, deseeded and diced
1 green pepper, deseeded and diced
1 yellow pepper, deseeded and diced
1 red onion, diced
1 red chilli, deseeded, minced
1 green chilli, deseeded and minced

1tbs flat leaf parsley, finely chopped
2 tbs chives, chopped
4 tbs olive oil
2 garlic gloves, minced
1tbs grated ginger
2tsp sea salt
1tsp ground black pepper

Method:
1. Grill sweetcorn, this can be done on a BBQ or under the grill of your cooker.
2. This should take about 8 minutes to create that browned colour, turning on each side to get an even colour.
3. Remove the corn from the cob by running a sharp knife down the cob. Set aside and keep warm.
4. Preheat oven to gas mark 7.
5. In a shallow baking tray, place peppers, onions, 2tbs olive oil, salt and pepper.
6. Toss all together and roast in oven for 30 minutes until tender.
7. Combine roast corn and peppers. Place a saucepan on a medium heat, add remainder of olive oil, minced red and green chilli, fry for 1minute to soften.
8. Add ginger and garlic saute' for a further 1 minute, stirring to prevent burning.
9. Add roasted sweetcorn and peppers to chilli, garlic and ginger mix, stirring to allow all ingredient to be combined.
10. Remove from heat, toss in the parsley and chives and adjust seasoning.

Tip: This salad can be served warm or cold. Its also great with BBQ meats or fish.

St Lucian Salt Fish & Green Fig Salad   serves 4

This is a classic St Lucian dish we've eaten a lot of on our travels around the island. Green fig is another word for unripe bananas in the banana family. It's perfect for lunch or as a light starter and serve with freshley baked bread.

350g salt cod
4 green bananas
1 lime, cut in two
2 tbs olive oil
1 yellow bell pepper, diced
1 red chilli, diced
1 medium onion, chopped

4 spring onions, sliced
2 tsp fresh thyme leaves
2 tbs parsley, chopped
2 garlic cloves, minced
1/4 tsp ground black pepper
1 tsp Tan Rosie's Garlic & Pepper Sauce (HOT)
1 tbs fish sauce (optional)

Method for preparing the Salt Cod:

1. In a lidded container, place salt cod, add cold water and rinse thoroughly to remove some of the surface salt.
2. Add lime portions and more cold water to the salt cod, cover container and leave to soak overnight in fridge.
3. Next day, discard the water and add boiled water to cod, leave to continue to soak.
4. When water is cooled completely, discard water, remove bone and skin and flake cod.
5. Add boiled water to the flaked cod and leave to continue to rehydrate and desalinate cod for another hour.
6. Cod is now ready to use!

Method for preparing green bananas:

1. Top and tail green bananas and place in a saucepan with cold water and a sea salt.
2. Place on hob and bring to the boil, reduce heat and simmer for 10 minutes.
3. Remove the cooked green bananas and leave to cool.
4. When cooled, remove skins from bananas and cut into 1 inch thick slices and set aside.

Method for salad:

1. Place a saucepan on to hob on medium heat, add olive oil and chopped onions, saute for 10 minutes to soften onions until lightly golden.
2. Add minced garlic and saute for 1minute while stirring to prevent burning.
3. Add spring onions, chilli, bell peppers and thyme, stir and cook for 2 to 3 minutes.
4. Toss in the prepared salt cod, continue to stir, cook for a further 3 minutes.
5. Stir in hot sauce, fish sauce and chopped parsley.
6. Remove from heat, toss in the cooked bananas and serve.

jerk shrimp with roasted vegetable salad serves 4-6

We love this tasty shrimp salad. It's perfect for BBQ's or eat as a lovely lunch dish. Light, tasty and easy to make, try it!

For grilled jerk Prawns:
450g king prawns, if frozen, defrost or fresh prawns
Wooden skewers soaked in water for 30 minutes

For Marinade:
2 tbs olive oil
1 tbs fish sauce
1 lemon, juice and zest of
2 cloves garlic, minces
1/4 tsp sea salt
1/2 tsp ground black pepper
2 tsp Tan Rosie's Jerk Rub
2 tsp palm sugar or honey

Method:
1. In a mixing bowl, combine all the ingredients for the marinade and mix thoroughly.
2. Remove 2 tbs of the marinade and reserve for glazing salad later.
3. Add the prawns to the remainder marinade and toss together and leave to marinade for 5 to 10 minutes.
4. Thread the prawns unto skewers.
5. Using a grill pan on medium heat, grill prawns 2 minutes on either side.
6. Set aside to combine with roasted vegetables later.

For Roasted Vegetables:
1 Red bell pepper, diced into 1 inch pieces
1 Yellow bell pepper, diced into 1 inch pieces
1 large Courgette, diced into 1 inch pieces
1 medium red onion, diced
1 garlic clove thinly sliced
2 sweet corn, grilled separately, to be added to roasted vegetables later2 tbs olive oil
1 tsp sea salt
1 tsp ground black pepper

Method:
1. Preheat oven to gas mark 7.
2. In a Roasting tin combine all the above ingredients with the exception of the grilled corn, toss together until olive oil has coated all the vegetables.
3. Roast in oven on gas mark 7 for 35 minutes.
4. Remove the kernel from the sweet corn and add to roasted vegetables and toss together.
5. Remove the grilled prawns from skewers and add to roasted vegetables.
6. Add some of the reserved marinade to the mixture to taste.

Tip: Serve a flat bread of your choice e.g. Pitta bread, Roti or even a nice sour dough bread.

grilled chicken salad with rum & lime vinaigrette

Tastes great on a sunny afternoon, this salad tastes sublime! Juicy grilled chicken teamed with our delicious rum and lime vinaigrette is heavenly. Try it.

For Chicken:
2 chicken breasts, cut into 2" cubes
1 tbs olive oil
1/2 tsp sea salt
1/2 tsp ground black pepper
1 tsp Tan Rosie Garlic & Pepper Sauce (Hot)
1 lime, juice and zest
Cooking oil spray, e.g. Canola oil

Chicken Method:
1. In small dish combine olive oil, sea salt. Black pepper and hot sauce to create a paste.
2. In another bowl put cubed chicken breast and rub in paste.
3. Cover and set aside in fridge to marinade for at least 2 hours.
4. Spray griddle pan with cooking oil, place on medium heat.
5. When pan is hot, place cubed chicken, cook for 5 minutes then turn chicken.
6. Continue cooking for a further 5 minutes, turn off heat and allow to rest, covered with foil.

For Rum and Lime Vinaigrette Dressing:
6 tbs light olive oil
1/2 tsp sea salt
1/4 tsp ground black pepper
1 tbs rum
1 tbs white wine vinegar
1 tbs honey
Zest of 1 lime
1 tbs lime juice

Salad Method:
1. In a screw top jar, place all the above ingredients and shake well.
2. Dressing can be kept in the fridge for up to a week.
3. Serve grilled chicken and dressing with a salad of your choice.

bbq pork mango salad

Pork and mango are lovely combination. This is a delicious bbq pork dish for summer parties and meal. Great for all the family too. Serve with crusty bread or a light cous cous salad.

Pork Ingredients:
4 Pork shoulder steaks
1tbs olive oil
1tbs soya sauce
1tbs Worcestershire sauce
1tsp ground black pepper

1 scotch bonnet pepper, deseeded and minced
1tsp ground allspice
1/2tsp sea salt
2tsp vegetable stock powder or 1 stock cube crumbled
2tsp fresh thyme leaves

Method:

1. In a lidded container, place pork steaks in another container or bowl, place all the other ingredients and mix well, creating a marinade.

2. Rub the marinade into the pork steaks, ensuring meat is fully covered.

3. Cover and leave to marinade for at least 2 hours or overnight preferable in the fridge.

4. To cook in oven, preheat oven to gas mark 7.

5. In a roasting tray, place marinated pork with all the marinade, cover with foil and roast for 30 minutes.

6. After 30 minutes remove foil and continue to roast open for a further 15 to 20 minutes.

7. Remove from oven cover with foil to rest before slicing thinly for the salad.

Tip: For a BBQ flavour the pork can be finished off on the BBQ and grill for 8 to 10 minutes!

Mango Salad:
1 large firm mango, peeled and diced
1 Red pepper, deseeded, and diced
1 Green pepper, deseeded and diced
3 stalks of spring onions, chopped
1 small red onion, diced finely

1 tbs fresh parsley, finely chopped
1tbs fresh coriander, finely chopped
2 red chilli, deseeded and minced
1tbs lemon juice
1tsp sea salt
1/2tsp ground black pepper
1tbs olive oil

Method:

1. In a mixing bowl, place the first 8 ingredients and toss together.

2. In a lidded bottle, put the next 4 ingredients and shake well to make a dressing.

3. Add dressing to other ingredients and toss together to mix.

4. Serve with pork.

yam & sweet potato salad

A great twist on the traditional potato salad with lovely Caribbean ingredients. Add a dash of hot sauce for extra kick!

400g yam, diced
400g white sweet potato, diced
2 spring onions, chopped
1/4 cup parsley, chopped
1 green chilli, deseeded and finely
minced
1 cup mayonnaise
1/4 cup sour cream
1 tbs white wine vinegar
1 tbs capers, chopped
1 tsp Tan Rosie's Garlic & Pepper
Sauce (HOT)
1tsp sea salt
1/2 tsp ground black pepper

Method:
1. Peel and dice the yam and sweet potato.
2. Boil in salted water for 10 to 12 minutes until tender.
3. Drain and place yam and sweet potato in a large mixing bowl.
4. Add spring onions, chilli and capers to mixing bowl with the potatoes and yams and toss together.
5. In another bowl combine mayonnaise, sour cream, white wine vinegar, garlic and pepper sauce, sea salt and black pepper and mix well to make the sauce for the potato and yam.
6. Add the sauce to potato and yam mixture and gently mix to combine.
7. Can be served warm or at room temperature.

Tip: A firm white sweet potato is recommended for this salad.

desserts

chocolate & ginger cake

This flourless chocolate cake is made with tasty almonds. It's incredibly moreish and decadent, decorated with juicy ginger pieces and a lovely layer of chocolate. This truly is chocolate heaven!

200g ground almonds
4 large eggs, separated
180g soft light brown sugar
80g grated dark chocolate, at least 70%
120g grated stem ginger
2 tbs stem ginger syrup (the syrup from your stem ginger)
2 tsp coffee blended with 2tsp hot water and cooled
1 tsp ground cinnamon
1/4 tsp grated nutmeg
1 tsp ginger extract
1/4 tsp salt

Topping Ingredients:
150 mls soured cream
5 oz dark chocolate
1 tbs Soft light brown sugar
2 pieces of stem ginger, sliced thinly, for decoration

Method:

1. Preheat oven to gas mark 4. Grease a 9 inch cake with some butter and line the base of tin with a circle grease proof paper.
2. In a bowl, using an electric mixer if possible, cream the egg yolks with 1/2 the sugar until light and fluffy.
3. In another bowl, again using an electric mixer if possible, place the egg whites and adding a little sugar at a time whisk until soft peaks is achieved.
4. To the bowl with the egg yolks add the ground almonds, grated chocolate, grated stem ginger, cinnamon, nutmeg, syrup of ginger, coffee, ginger extract and salt. Mix well.
5. Add a third of the egg white to the chocolate mixture and mix using a metal spoon. Fold in the remainder of egg white. Pour batter into cake tin.
6. Bake in oven for 50 to 60 minutes. After 50 minutes insert skewer into cake, if the skewer comes out clean the cake is cooked. If not clean return to oven to continue the cooking process.
7. When cooked leave to cool for 10 minutes then turn out cake on rack.

Topping Method:

1. Place a saucepan with water onto a medium heat. In a bowl, place dark chocolate and sugar and melt stirring over the saucepan of simmering water, add soured cream and continue to mix well until thoroughly blended.
2. Leave to cool. Using a palette knife spread mixture over cake. Place topping over cake.
3. Leave to set in fridge until ready to use.

coconut & cinnamon rolls

makes 24

Coconut is a popular ingredient in the Caribbean which can be used across many dishes. We've teamed it with cinnamon to form these beautiful rolls. We think they are best served warm with a cuppa!

Dough Ingredients:

500g Strong plain flour
100g butter
50g vegetable shortening
80g sugar
10g yeast
1 tsp sea salt
300mls Warm Milk and water mix

Dough Method:

1. In mixing bowl, place first 6 ingredients and rub in.
2. Add the milk and water blend a little at a time to form a soft dough.
3. Turn out onto a floured surface and knead for 10 to 15 minutes.
4. Return to mixing bowl, cover with cling film or a damp clean tea towel in a warm place for 1 hour or until doubled in size.

Filling Ingredients:

2 cups freshly grated coconut
1 Tbs grated ginger
1 cup sugar
1/4 tsp ground Allspice
1/2 tsp ground cinnamon
1/4 tsp ground cloves
1/4 tsp ground cloves
1/4 tsp grated nutmeg
1/4 tsp sea salt
1/2 cup water
2 tsp vanilla extract
2 Tbs honey
Zest of 1 lime

Filling Method:

1. Place all ingredients, except vanilla extract, in a saucepan and put onto a medium heat. Bring to the boil and simmer for 10 to 15 minutes. Stirring occasionally, It should reduce to a slightly sticky consistency.
2. Remove pan from heat source, stir in vanilla extract.
3. Set aside and leave to cool before using.

Syrup Glaze Ingredients:

100g melted butter
1 cup soft brown sugar
1/4 cup ground cinnamon

Rolls Method:

1. Knead dough, divide dough into 2. Roll out each section into 1 centimetre and 16"rectangle
2. Brush rolled dough with melted butter, sprinkle with sugar and cinnamon and spread the coconut mixture on top.
3. Roll the dough and coconut into a sausage shape, cut into 12 portions.
4. Place on greased baking tray. Cover with a damp clean tea cloth and leave to proof for 1 hour.
5. Repeat the above process with the other section of dough.
6. After 1 hour preheat oven on gas mark 6.
7. Place rolls in oven 50 to 60 minutes or until cooked
8. When cooked/baked brush tops rolls with sugar syrup glaze and leave to cool on a wire rack.

cinnamon shortbread

We've often made cinnamon shortbread to accompany our favourite ice creams at our Supper Clubs. It adds a lovely crunch and extra flavour to silky smooth ice cream. Tastes just as good with a lovely cup of tea too!

4 oz butter, softened
2 oz cornflour
4 oz plain flour
2 oz caster sugar
1 tsp ground cinnamon
Pinch of sea salt
Castor sugar for dusting

Method:
1. Preheat oven to gas mark 4. In a mixing bowl, cream butter and sugar.
2. Sift flour, cinnamon and sea salt into butter and sugar mixture, blend together to form smooth paste.
3. Collect up dough into a ball and wrap in cling film and refrigerate for 10 minutes to firm up.
4. Roll out dough between 2 sheets of cling film.
5. Using a fluted 21/2" pastry cutter or any shapes of your choice.
6. Place some parchment paper onto a baking tray, arrange shortbread on parchment.
7. Using a for prick each shortbread through, sprinkle with caster sugar and cinnamon.
8. Bake in oven on gas mark 4 for 20 to 25 minutes until slightly golden brown.
9. Leave on baking parchment for 10 minutes and then place on a wire rack to cool completely.

Great with ice cream!

coconut tart

Every Caribbean island has it's own version of a coconut tart. If you go into any bakery from Grenada to St Lucia you will find some fantastic coconut tarts, breads or pastries. This tart is amazing with a dollop of double cream or ice cream.

Short crust Pastry:
4 oz Plain flour
2 oz butter cut into cubes
2-3 Tbsp cold water
pinch of salt
8" pastry dish

For filling:
250g grated coconut
200g Dates chopped
1/2 cup light brown sugar
1/4 cup Maple syrup
1/4 cup water
1/4 tsp ground cinnamon
1/4 tsp ground allspice
1/4 tsp ground nutmeg
1 tsp vanilla extract

Pastry Method:
1. In mixing bowl place flour, cubed butter and salt.
2. Rub butter into four until it resembles fine bread crumbs.
3. Add cold water a little at a time, drawing all ingredients together to form a dough.
4. Wrap pastry in cling film, refrigerate for 15 to 20 minutes until ready to use.
5. On a floured board roll out pastry to the thickness of a pound coin.
6. Place rolled pastry into pastry dish.
7. Place greaseproof paper over pastry add baking beans and blind bake for 10 to 15 minutes on gas mark 7, then cool.

Tip: Ready made pastry will work very well!

Filling Method:
1. Place all ingredients, except vanilla extract, in a saucepan.
2. Place on low to medium heat and slowly bring to boil.
3. Turn heat down to simmer and cook for 5 to 8 minutes stirring occasionally.
4. Remove from heat and stir in vanilla extract.
5. Leave to cool.
6. Spread filling into pastry case.
7. Bake at gas mark 6 for 20 minutes.
8. Serve warm with a vanilla ice cream or double cream.

monica's rum cake

serves up to 12

You can't beat a good old fashioned rum cake in the Caribbean! We love eating our rum cake slightly warm with a dollop of double cream or lashings of custard, yummy!

Fruit Mixture Ingredients:
1 kg seedless raisins
500g currants
250g dried cherries
250g dates
125g mixed citrus peel
2 cups cherry brandy
1 cup dark rum
2 tsp cinnamon
3 tsp vanilla extract

Method:

1. Using a food processor, place all ingredients in bowl, blend to coarse consistency.

2. In a lidded sterilised jar, put all the blended fruit, cover and leave in a cool dry place for at least one week or up to a year.

3. Tip a Kilner Jar will be ideal for this.

Ingredients For Cake:
2 cups self raising flour
3 cups fruit mixture
250g softened butter
250g soft brown sugar
6 eggs
2 tsp baking powder

2 tsp ground cinnamon
1 tsp ground allspice
1/2 tsp grated nutmeg
2 tsp vanilla extract
200g ground almonds
1/2 tsp sea salt
1/2 cup dark rum
1/4 cup cherry brandy

Ingredients for basting on completion of baking
1/2 cup cherry brandy
1/2 cup dark rum

Method:

1. Grease 2 9" cake tins

2. Preheat oven to gas mark 5

3. Using an electric mixer, cream butter and sugar in large mixing bowl until light and fluffy.

4. Add eggs one at a time and beat into butter mixture.

5. Add fruit mixture to egg and creamed butter mix until fully dispersed in.

6. Add rum, cherry brandy, vanilla extract and stir.

7. Add ground almonds, flour, baking powder, cinnamon, allspice, nutmeg and salt and fold in until all the dry ingredients are blended without over working the batter.

8. Pour batter into cake tins, place oven for 1 1/4 hours.

9. Next after 1 1/4 hours insert a skewer into cake, if skewer comes out clean, cake is cooked. If not return to oven and continue cooking until done.

10. Remove from oven, leave for 20 minutes to cool.

11. Brush cherry brandy and rum mixture over cake.

12. Leave cake to cool completely.

13. Wrap in cling film and then in foil and in a lidded container. Store in cool dry place.

14. Leave cake for at least 3 days before consuming.

pecan pie

We served this thing of beauty up at a special Soul Food themed Supper Club.
Needless to say it all went pretty quickly!

For Pastry:
8 oz plain flour
1/4 tsp sea salt
2 oz vegetable shortening
3 0oz butter
2 tsp caster sugar
1/4 cup iced water to combine

For Filling:
1 1/2 lbs pecan nuts
4 large eggs
8 oz light brown sugar
6 oz Maple syrup
1/2 tsp sea salt
2 oz butter, melted
1 tsp Vanilla extract
1/4 cup Dark rum
2 tbs corn flour

Method:

1. Preheat oven to gas mark 7 and place a baking tray in oven.
2. In a mixing bowl add plain flour, salt, shortening and butter. Rub these ingredients together until it resembles fine bread crumbs.
3. Add the sugar and mix through.
4. Add the water and combine to make a firm dough.
5. Wrap in cling film and rest in fridge for 10 minutes.
6. Remove from fridge and roll out pastry to fit into an 11 inch pastry dish.
7. Leave to rest for 15 minutes in fridge.
8. Bake the pastry blind, line pastry with greaseproof paper and fill with dried or ceramic beans and bake until the sides are cooked.
9. Remove the greaseproof paper with the beans and continue cooking the pastry until done.
10. While the pastry is being cooked, make the filling.
11. Pan roast half of the pecan nuts, the remainder will be used as the topping for the pie.
12. Using a frying pan add the nuts and place on a medium heat and roast for a short while until nuts are slightly coloured.
13. Remove from pan onto a chopping board and roughly chop. In a mixing bowl, whisk the eggs, add the sugar, maple syrup, melted butter, sea salt and vanilla extract and mix well together.
14. Combine the rum with the cornflour and add to the mixture and continue mixing well.
15. Add the chopped nuts and mix through.
16. Pour the mixture into the blind baked pastry case then arrange the remainder of the pecan nuts on top.
17. Bake on the hot baking tray for 10 minutes at gas mark 6 then turn oven temperature down to gas mark 3 and cook for a further 40 to 45 minutes or until pie is just set.

Tip: This pie can be served warm with cream or ice cream.

mango ice cream

We love mangoes, so teaming it with ice cream is a dream! It's very moreish, creamy, decadent and very easy to make too. Try with cinnamon shortbread on the side.

500ml good quality ready made custard
150g castor sugar
1tin condensed milk
500ml double cream
2 tsp vanilla extract
1 tsp grated nutmeg
1/2 tsp ground cinnamon
500g mango, pureed

Method:
1. Using a kitchen maid and a whisk attachment, whip together, double cream, custard, sugar, condensed milk, vanilla extract until light and fluffy.
2. Stir in the mango puree.
3. Pour into a lidded container and freeze until ready for use.

Tip: Other electric whisk can be used. Remove ice cream from freezer at least 10 minutes before serving.

lime & ginger cheesecake

Classic Caribbean ingredients transform the humble cheesecake. It tastes as good as it looks folks. Enjoy!

300g ginger biscuits, crushed finely
100g butter, melted
900g soft cream cheese
200g caster sugar
200ml sour cream
2 limes, juice and zest of
200g stem ginger, chopped
4 eggs + 1 egg yolk
2 tsp vanilla extract
1/2 cup plain flour
Pinch of sea salt

For Topping:
200g white chocolate
2 tbs sour cream
1 lime, juice and zest

For Garnish:
6 thinly slices of lime
3 tbs finely chopped stem ginger
2 tsp lime zest

10 inch spring form cake tin

Method:

1. Preheat oven to gas mark 6.
2. In a mixing bowl combine the crumbed ginger biscuits and melted butter.
3. Press into the spring form cake tin, bake in oven for 10 to 12 minutes.
4. Remove from oven and leave to cool while the cheesecake filling is prepared.
5. In the a large mixing bowl cream the cream cheese and sugar until fluffy, an electric mixer would be ideal for this process.
6. Add sour cream, juice and lime zest, vanilla extract, ginger and mix through.
7. Add the eggs one at a time and mix thoroughly.
8. Sift in the flour and salt and stir well to incorporate.
9. Pour mixture into cake tin. Place cheesecake on a baking tray and bake at gas mark 4 for 1 hour 15 minutes.
10. Turn oven off and leave cake in oven to cool for at least 4 hours.
11. Leave to chill in fridge for at least 6 hours or over night.

To prepare topping:

1. Place a saucepan with hot water on medium heat.
2. In a mixing bowl, put white chocolate, broken in pieces, sour cream, zest and juice of lime.
3. Stir over the simmering boiling water to melt chocolate and to combine all the ingredients to a smooth consistency.
4. Set aside to cool before spreading on to chilled cheesecake.
5. After spreading on topping leave to cool completely in fridge.
6. Just before serving decorate with the above garnish.

peanut brittle

Peanut brittle is called "peanut cake" in the Caribbean. It's popular dessert snack found in many homes and market stalls across the islands. For an extra twist, we've added bicarbonate of soda and stem ginger.

2 cups roasted peanuts
1 1/2 cups granulated sugar
1/3 cup water
1/3 cup stem ginger, finely diced
1/4 cup syrup from stem ginger
1/4 tsp ground cinnamon
1/4 tsp ground allspice
1 tsp bicarbonate of soda
Pinch of sea salt

Method:
1. Prepare a baking tray by lining with a sheet of baking parchment.
2. Place a saucepan on a medium heat, add water, ginger syrup and sugar, boil to a soft ball consistency.
3. Add cinnamon, allspice and stem ginger and stir.
4. Add bicarbonate of soda and peanuts and stir. Turn out the peanut and ginger mixture on to baking tray and spread out.
5. Sprinkle with a little sea salt and allow cake to cool down.
6. Break up into pieces before serving when cold.

drinks

guinness punch

Guinness punch is a classic drink consumed across many Caribbean islands. We love the use of sweet spices and delicious condensed milk to sweeten.

500ml Guinness Stout
2 cups Condensed Milk
1 tsp Vanilla extract
Pinch ground Cinnamon
Pinch Grated Nutmeg
Ice to serve

Method:
1. In a large jug, place all the above ingredients and stir well to combine.
2. Pour over ice cubes in tall glasses and serve.

mango, pineapple & coconut smoothie   serves 4-6

Smoothies are a great breakfast boost and you can't beat this tasty combination to start you off for the day.

1 large Mango, deseeded and
diced or
2 cups frozen mango chunks
1/2 Fresh pineapple, peeled and
cut into cubes or
2 cups frozen pineapple chunks
1 tbs grated fresh ginger
1tbs honey or Maple syrup
1tsp vanilla Extract
4 drops Angostura Bitters
Pinch of ground cinnamon
1 cup coconut water
Ice to serve

Method:
1. Place all the ingredients into a blender and blitz until smooth.
2. Serve over ice.

sorrel juice

Another Caribbean classic! Sorrel is a flower grown all over the Caribbean available in white or red. The flower is dried then processed into a delicious drink. It's normally drank around Christmas time. Also tastes great with rum!

1 pk dried Sorrel petals
100g grated ginger
3 litres water
3 lemons - juice and rind
3 cups sugar
2 cinnamon sticks
ice and rum to serve

Method:
1. In preserving pan/saucepan add sorrel, ginger, water, lemon rind, sugar, and cinnamon sticks.
2. Place on heat and bring to the boil, then turn heat down and simmer for 15 minutes.
3. Remove off the heat, add lemon juice, cover pan and leave to cool.
4. Strain and pass through a muslin cloth.
5. Place in sterilised bottles and store in the fridge.
6. Best serve with lots of ice and perhaps a little rum!

tamarind juice

Tamarind is a fruit grown on large trees across the Caribbean and many other tropical countries. It's got a sweet and sour flavour and can be enjoyed in sweet and savoury dishes. It's fabulous as a drink too!

1 pack Tamarind paste, rehydrated with 500mls water
100g grated ginger
4 litres water
3 lemons - juice and rind
3 cups granulated sugar
2 cinnamon sticks
ice to serve
1 Litre bottles x 4
Muslin cloth

Method:
1. Sieve the tamarind paste into a preserving pan/saucepan and discard the seeds and pulp.
2. Add the remainder of the water, grated ginger, rind of lemons, sugar and cinnamon sticks.
3. Place pan on high heat and bring to the boil, turn heat down to a low heat and simmer for 15 minutes.
4. Remove from heat source.
5. Add lemon juice, Cover with cling film and allow to cool.
6. When cooled strain through a double layer of muslin/cheesecloth.
7. Store in sterilised bottles in fridge until ready to use.
8. Serve with lots of ice and maybe some Rum!

Tips:
1. Makes at least 4 litres.
2. Great for Summer parties or any celebration.

pineapple & rum punch

Pineapple and rum are a winning combination for this perfect punch on warm sunny days. If you're having a BBQ party, then this will go down a treat with your loved ones.

2 cups pineapple juice
1 cup rum
1/2 cup simple sugar syrup
2 limes/lemons, juice of
6 drops Angustura Bitters
pinch grated nutmeg
2 cups Ice cubes
Pineapple slices to garnish

Method:
1. In a large jug combine all the above ingredients and stir.
2. Serve in tall glasses with a slice of pineapple.

menu ideas

caribbean menus

We've been running our Caribbean Supper Club for 6 years and we've enjoyed cooking and hosting for hundreds of guests in our living room.

It's a great chance for us to experiment with new ideas and twists on traditional recipes. We always make time to travel to as many Caribbean islands to learn new dishes, chat to the locals about their family meals and of course to eat as much tasty food as possible!

Here are a selection of our most recent Supper Club menus which feature different cuisines from across the Caribbean.

It's a great way to help you to organise and plan your meals for your family and friends.

Enjoy cooking!

Tan Rosie Caribbean Supper Club

Caribbean Classics

Appetizer
Plantain Crisps with Sweet Chilli Sauce &
Complimentary Ginger Drink (virgin)
&
Homemade Bread Rolls

Starter
Jerk Chicken Wings
or
(v) Corn Fritters
Main
Curry Mutton

or
(v) Monica's Ital Stew

Sides
Seasonal Vegetables, Fried Plantain
Dessert
Traditional Run Fruit Cake with Vanilla
Custard
or
Fresh Fruit Salad

Drinks
Tea/Coffee/Water/Bring Your Own Alcohol

Dominican ==Republic

Appetizer
Plantain Crisps with Mango Sauce & Complimentary Ginger Drink (virgin)
&
Homemade Bread Rolls

Starter
Kipes (Bulgur wheat stuffed with minced beef)
or
(v) Kipes (Bulgur wheat stuffed with mushrooms)

Main
Pollo Guisado (stewed chicken)

or
(v) Plantain & Red Bean Curry

Sides
Arroz Blanco (white rice), **Yucca con Cebolla** (cassava & onions)

Dessert
Vanilla & White Chocolate & Raspberry Cheesecake with Raspberry Sauce
or
Fresh Fruit Salad

Drinks
Tea/Coffee/Water/Bring Your Own Alcohol

Tan Rosie Caribbean Supper Club
Grenada
Spice Isl

Appetizer
Plantain Crisps with Mango Sauce & Complimentary
Ginger Drink (virgin)
&
Homemade Bread Rolls

Starter
Salt Fish 'n' Bakes
or
(v) Corn Fritters

Main
Carriacou Stewed Pork
or
(v) Belvedere Breadfruit Pie

Sides
Rolled White Rice, Rolled Coo Coo, Seasonal Veg
Dessert
Nutmeg Ice Cream with Homemade Cinnamon
Shortbread
or
Fresh Fruit Salad

Drinks
Tea/Coffee/Water/Bring Your Own Alcohol

Tan Rosie Caribbean Supper Club

Kingston Jamaica Cook-up

Appetizer
Plantain Crisps with Jerk Red Pepper Sauce & Complimentary Ginger Drink (virgin)
&
Homemade Bread Rolls

Starter
Traditional Beef Patties
or
(v) Veggie Patties

Main
Classic Brown Stew Chicken
or
(v) Ital Stew

Sides
Rice & Peas, Seasonal Vegetables, Fried Plantain
Dessert
Zingy Ginger Cake with Cream
or
Fresh Fruit Salad

Drinks
Tea/Coffee/Water/Bring Your Own Alcohol

Tan Rosie Caribbean Supper Club

Jerk Extravaganza!

Appetizer
Plantain Crisps with Tamarind Sauce & Complimentary
Ginger Drink (virgin)
&
Jamaican Style Fried Bakes

Starter
Accras (contains Salt Fish) with **Jerk Pepper Sauce (mild)**
or
(v) **Corn Fritters**

Main
Jerk Red Snapper & Jerk Chicken
or
(v) Coo Coo (polenta) with sauted veg and Red pepper
Sauce

Sides
Sauted Cassava Mash, Seasonal Vegetables, Rice

Dessert
Dark Rum & Chocolate Cake with Cream
or
Fresh Fruit Salad

Drinks
Tea/Coffee/Water/Bring Your Own Alcohol

Tan Rosie **Caribbean Supper Club**

Martinique

Appetizer
Chips de Plantain et Sauce de Tamarin & Complimentary Ginger Drink (virgin)
&
Rouleaux de Bréal Maison (Homemade Bread Rolls)

Starter
Accras (fish)
or
(v) Beignets de Maïs (corn fritters)

Main
Chicken Columbo (chicken curry)

or
(v) Citrouille et Christophine Gratin (pumpkin and christophene gratin)

Sides
Plantain Cuit a la Vapeur, Riz Blanc, Legumes de Saison

Dessert
Gâteau à la Banane à la Sauce au Rhum
or
Fresh Fruit Salad

Drinks
Tea/Coffee/Water/Bring Your Own Alcohol

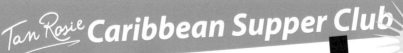

St Lucia

Appetizer
Plantain Crisps with Mango Sauce & Complimentary
Sorrel Drink (virgin)
&
Homemade Bread Rolls

Starter
St Lucian Dhal with Salt Fish
or
(v) St Lucian Dhal with Split Pea & Roasted Veg

Main
Curry Chicken Roti
or
(v) Curry Veg Roti

Sides
Seasonal Vegetables, Meldey of Ground Provisions

Dessert
Coconut Tart with Rum Cream
or
Fresh Fruit Salad

Drinks
Tea/Coffee/Water/Bring Your Own Alcohol

Tan Rosie Caribbean Supper Club

Caribbean Surf & Turf

Appetizer
Plantain Crisps with Mango Sauce & Complimentary
Ginger Drink (virgin)

Starter
Juicy Corn Fritters with BBQ Tamarind Sauce

Main
Jerk Shrimp & Jerk Belly Pork Skewers with Sweet Red
Pepper Sauce
or
(v) Monica's 3 Bean Stew

Sides
Sweet Potato Balls, Rice, Seasonal Vegetables, Fried
Plantain

Dessert
Mango & Passionfruit Cheesecake
or
Fresh Fruit Salad

Drinks
Tea/Coffee/Water/Bring Your Own Alcohol

Tan Rosie Caribbean Supper Club
Trini Curry Nite

Appetizer
Plantain Crisps with Chilli Lime Sauce & Complimentary
Ginger Drink (virgin)
&
Homemade Bread Rolls

Starter
Crab & Callaloo Fritters with Tamarind Sauce
or
(v) Callaloo Fritters with Tamarind Sauce

Main
Trini Curry Chicken
or
(v) Sweet Potato & Eggplant Curry

Sides
Buss-Up-Shut (Roti), Rice, Mango & Ginger Chutney
Dessert
Pineapple & Cinnamon Cake with Cream
or
Fresh Fruit Salad

Drinks
Tea/Coffee/Water/Bring Your Own Alcohol

glossary

weights & measurements

Gas Mark	Fahrenheit	Celsius	Description
1/4	225	110	Very cool/very slow
1/2	250	130	---
1	275	140	cool
2	300	150	---
3	325	170	---
4	350	180	---
5	375	190	---
6	400	200	moderate
7	425	220	hot
8	450	230	---
9	475	240	very hot

1 tablespoon (tbsp) =	3 teaspoons (tsp)
1/16 cup =	1 tablespoon
1/8 cup =	2 tablespoons
1/6 cup =	2 tablespoons + 2 teaspoons
1/4 cup =	4 tablespoons
1/3 cup =	5 tablespoons + 1 teaspoon
3/8 cup =	6 tablespoons
1/2 cup =	8 tablespoons
2/3 cup =	10 tablespoons + 2 teaspoons
3/4 cup =	12 tablespoons
1 cup =	150gm
8 fluid ounces (fl oz) =	1 cup
1 pint (pt) =	2 cups
1 quart (qt) =	2 pints
4 cups =	1 quart
1 gallon (gal) =	4 quarts
16 ounces (oz) =	1 pound (lb)
1 milliliter (ml) =	1 cubic centimeter (cc)
1 inch (in) =	2.54 centimeters (cm)

Capacity		Weight	
1/5 teaspoon	1 milliliter	1 oz	28 grams
1 teaspoon	5 ml	1 pound	454 grams
1 tablespoon	15 ml		
1 fluid oz	30 ml		
1/5 cup	47 ml		
1 cup	237 ml		
2 cups (1 pint)	473 ml		
4 cups (1 quart)	.95 liter		
4 quarts (1 gal.)	3.8 liters		

index

index

a

ackee & salt fish tart 104
aubergine
  aubergine, sweet potato & spinach curry 114
  stuffed aubergines 118

b

bakery 36
bread
  monica's cornbread 54
  cassava bread 52
  onion flat bread with chilli 46
  banana bread 48
  homemade bread rolls 44
beef
  caribbean beef stew 82
  Jamaican beef patties 78
  dominican republic beef kipes 77
beans
  spiced 3 bean stew & dumplings 122
  Jamaican style rice & peas 134
bbq
  bbq pork mango salad 154
  monica's bbq jerk chicken 80
  jerk bbq ribs with sweet chilli lime glaze 72
  slow roast bbq belly pork 88
banana
  st lucian salt fish & green fig salad 148
  banana bread 48

c

caribbean fruit & vegetables 9
essential caribbean cooking tips 33
Corn
  monica's cornbread 54
  roasted corn & sweet pepper salad 146
  coo coo poi 128
coconut
  coconut scones 50
  roasted butternut squash & coconut soup 62
  coconut & callaloo rice 142
  coconut tart 166
  pineapple, mango & coconut smoothie 181
  coconut & cinnamon rolls 162
cassava
  cassava bread 52
  crushed cassava & garlic mash 136
callaloo
  callaloo & crab soup 60
  coconut & callaloo rice 142
  callaloo fritters 138
  caramalised onion & callaloo patties 120
  creole callaloo, spinach & prawn tart 98

chicken
  monica's fried chicken 86
  monica's bbq jerk chicken 80
  pollo guisado 74
  caribbean lime roast chicken 70
  grilled chicken salad with rum & lime vinaigrette 152
curry
  trini prawn curry 102
  aubergine, sweet potato & spinach curry 114
  jamaican beef patties 78
  veggie curry patties 110
cous cous
  pumpkin cous cous salad 140
christophene
  st lucian christophene & roast pumpkin gratin 116
cakes
  monica's spiced rum cake 168
  chocolate & ginger cake 160
crab
  crab fritters 94
  callaloo & crab soup 60

d

dumplings
  callaloo & crab soup 60
  fried bakes (dumplings) 38
desserts 158
dominican republic menu 192
drinks 178

f

festivals 40
fritters
  callaloo fritters 138
  crab fritters 94
fish dishes 91
  jerk shrimp & roasted vegetable salad 150
  st lucian salt fish & green fig salad 148

g

ginger
  lime & ginger cheesecake 174
  chocolate & ginger cake 160
guiness punch 180
grenada menu 193

j

jerk
jerk bbq ribs with sweet chilli lime glaze 72
monica's bbq jerk chicken 80
jerk shrimp & roasted vegetable salad 150
jamaican menu

l

lime
caribbean lime roast chicken 70
lime & ginger cheesecake 174
jerk bbq ribs with sweet chilli lime glaze 72
grilled chicken salad with rum & lime
vinaigrette 152

m

mango
mango ice cream 172
bbq pork mango salad 154
pineapple, mango & coconut smoothie 181
mutton
traditional mutton soup 64
spiced slow roast leg of mutton 84
menus

o

onion
caramalised onion & callaloo patties 120
onion flat bread with chilli 46
oxtail
oxtail soup 63
okra
deep fried okra 130

p

pecan pie 170
plantain
pan fried plantain with a polenta crust 132
pineapple
pineapple, mango & coconut smoothie 181
pineapple & rum punch 186
pumpkin
st lucian christophene & roasted pumpkin gratin
116
pumpkin muffins 56
roasted pumpkin tart with feta cheese 108
pumpkin cous cous 140
pumpkin muffins 56
pork
slow roast bbq belly pork 88
jerk bbq ribs with sweet chilli lime glaze 72
peanut

r

rice
coconut & callaloo rice 142
jamaican style rice & peas 134
vegetable lokri 124
rum
pineapple rum punch 186
monica's rum cake 168
roti
dhal puri roti 43

s

soup
traditional mutton soup 64
callaloo & crab soup 60
pigeon pea soup 66
roasted butternut squash & coconut soup 62
oxtail soup 63
salads 144
smoothies
pineapple, mango & coconut smoothie 181
stews
spiced 3 bean stew & dumplings 122
scones
coconut scones 50
st lucian menu 197
sorrel juice 182

t

tamarind
tamarind juice 184
trinidad
trinidad & tobago classics menu 199
trini prawn curry 102

v

vegetarian dishes 106

y

yam
yam & sweet potato salad 156